THE HOUSE AT BLAZO'S CORNER
A ghost story

by
Mary Freeman

Shedchamber Press
11 Ataraxian Access
Monroe, Maine 04951
mfreeman@gmail.com
(207) 322-3034

FLORA VISITS PARSONSFIELD

A poem about the house at Blazo's Corner seen through the eyes of
Mimi Hanson, circa 1953
by Mary Freeman (aka Mimi Hanson)

Flora is the protagonist of *The Gardens of Flora Baum,* an epic poem in five books
by Julia Budenz. *Flora Visits Parsonsfield* records an anachronistic encounter between
the ghost of Mimi Hanson, circa 1953, and Flora.

Dedicated to my mother Constance Ruggli Leavitt Hanson
(b. Dec. 19, 1907-- d. April 8, 1998)

Mary (Polly) Freeman Blazo Aug 1, 1812—Aug. 22, 1900

RESIDENTS OF THE HOUSE, 1812-1973

William Blazo Mar 1, 1777—Aug 25, 1830
Mehitable Wedgewood Blazo May 10, 1786—July 24, 1862
Robert Tibbetts Blazo Aug. 11, 1797—May 24, 1890
Mary (Polly) Freeman Blazo Aug 1, 1812—Aug. 22, 1900
Susan French Freeman Cooke May 22, 1783—August 22, 1844
Lott Cooke (stepfather of Mary (Polly) Freeman Blazo)
Daniel Otis Freeman Blazo Nov. 6, 1836—Aug. 22, 1914
Susan Chapman Blazo Leavitt Feb. 14, 1839—Feb. 13, 1920
John Greenleaf Leavitt Aug. 13, 1834--1885
Charles Blazo Aug. 3, 1842—Oct. 20, 1926
Emily Maria Blazo Browne Nov. 22, 1844—Oct. 19, 1924
Howard Hiram Browne, 1838--1897
Maude Browne June 7, 1867—Dec.4, 1932
Robert Greenleaf Leavitt Sept. 28, 1865—Oct. 2, 1942
Ella Janet Shumway Leavitt 1865—Feb 17, 1902
Robert Keith Leavitt Aug. 20, 1895—May, 1967
Russell Greenleaf Leavitt Dec. 19, 1896—Jan, 1984
Ida Gertrude Ruggli Leavitt, Oct. 8, 1872—July 1, 1958
Constance Ruggli Leavitt Hanson, Dec. 19, 1907—April 8, 1998
Hodge Jackson Hanson Oct, 1904-1997
Robert Jackson Hanson Dec. 3, 1936--Dec 16, 2011
Mary Freeman Hanson (aka Mimi Hanson) Nov. 11, 1943--
Ralph Bruce Wentworth, Aug. 1, 1936--
Eve Ruggli Wentworth July 23, 1963--
Rachael Chapman Wentworth Eastman, Oct. 9, 1965--
Donna Freeman Wentworth, Sept. 14, 1969--
Erika Hanson Wentworth Sept. 14, 1969--

SHED CHAMBER PRESS,
11 Ataraxian Access, Monroe, Maine 04951
mimi.freeman@gmail.com
First Printing, 2009
Second Printing, 2017
Second Edition 2021

("Come in, come in, dear Flora here come in! The hall/Is long and open here, and brings you to the stairs.")

FLORA VISITS PARSONSFIELD

Come in, come in, dear Flora here come in! The hall
Is long and open here, and brings you to the stairs.
The banister beckoning wants to take your hand--
It's had this whole long time your yearned-for visit planned.
And even Mimi, in from hunting mountain bears
Is waiting, hand pressed to the southwest parlor wall.

And though she wants to spring upstairs at once, she takes
You through the parlor door, where once her circus played
And shows you where the portraits hang, and how his eyes
Will follow you around the room, amused and wise.
The threadbare carpet here his Shaker mother made
Moves slowly with the shapes of shadowed snowflakes.

And Mimi pries open the old Emerson grand
To play for you a tune straight from her head (*High Noon)*
And opens up the cupboard door, so you see in
Wherein the china's kept, where lies her violin.
And there in the darkness glints an old silver spoon.
But on she wants to move--and hopes you'll understand

And yells "Come on upstairs!" and dashes out the room.
No time to show you out the window to the porch--
The porch she crawled out through the parlor window to.
We have to go upstairs, so much up there to show you!
Outside the parlor stands the hall and stairs, no torch
But sun required to light them; in light the hallway looms.

11

("Oh Flora, you must fly to follow! Mimi's fast/And leaps the sixteen steps in five quick bounds.")

Oh Flora, you must fly to follow! Mimi's fast
And leaps the sixteen steps in five quick bounds--she turns
And looks into the room due west and calls for you,
Still urging haste, to not let extra time accrue.
She has to show you Homer's bust, and all the urns,
The paint all petrified-- and feather mattress last.

And then the secret passage through the deep, deep closet;
The door is hidden, musty clothes are hanging in the way;
You have to push on through before you'll find yourself
Before the high-up chimney bookcase mantle-shelf
Atop the southwest bedroom's tall fireplace. I say
This for her, as she's still muffled in the closet,

("you'll find yourself/Before the high-up chimney bookcase mantle-

shelf/Atop the southwest bedroom's tall fireplace.")

Muffled and stopped by the close closet's hanging clothes
Which you must follow her through--on this she *insists,*
This obstinate girl in dungarees. And so you do
Go through the hidden door to get the promised view.
It's not so easily told of what that view consists
Green Mountain, upper branches of an elm tree; those

Golden window panes, the ambergris the hot sun
Gifted you in Summer; the thunder's rumble, rain
Pelting down on shingled roofs in tons, the great elm's
Swaying upper trunk, slow-tossing like a ship's helm.
Mimi remembers the sun's red glow and the pain
Of the elm disease, and sound of thundering tons.

And now you follow--Mimi's on the move again,
Right past the marble bureau-top and out the door,
Past the oaken desk, sit down on the window seat.
The hall ends there, where seat and wide-fanned window meet.
From there one sees the road, two hundred years or more
Ago, where Hampshire men drove by, cattle-herding then

Bound east for Portland's market--then the house was new.
Old Joe DeMarre, who made his way to Kezar Falls
In horse and wagon back in Nineteen Fifty-Three
Had waved and waved and waved to her, so she would see
And she waved back--Flora, can you hear him call?
He was very old. Old Joe was an Indian too.

There is a door across the hall, but Mimi runs.
She follows back the banister, then comes around
To where she's by the stairs again and stands--for here
Is where to stand to look, a distant spot not near
To see out through the fanning window span. No sound
She makes, but points instead to elm trees in the sun.

("...for here /Is where to stand to look, a distant spot not near /To
see out through the fanning window span.")

Across the road the elm's great spreading limbs are wide
Yet fit inside the window-frame's wide fan from here.
Please Flora in your book, find out for me or read
How those who framed the fan could know to sow the seed?
Or else ask Gaia, that ancient backwards-seer,
How came the world inside to fit the one outside?

Such questions she will ask some day, but cannot stop
To now; so follow Flora, Mimi's lead and keep
The answers in your head, she'll need them soon enough.
But now--right now--she has to show you other stuff--
Her mother' room, the cherry bed on which she'd leap
Up high to try and touch the ceiling stain, then drop

And try again, until she tired or else her mother came
And made her stop, and laughed at her, too nice
To even scold. And Mimi takes you in her room,
The little one just off her mother's own: its bloom
Of sunny light, this child's bedroom, must now entice
You to come in and sit beside its window frame.

(" And Mimi takes you in her room,/The little one just off her
mother's own...")

It faces east, this single-windowed room, and looks
Down on the granite steps beneath the tall east door
Which first you came in, Flora, coming through the hall.
And do you see that maple? (*Oh, hear Mimi call
Again to come!*) She wants to show you something more,
The northeast bedroom fireplace bookcase and its books.

Is this the third high-mantled fireplace that you've seen?
Let's see--the parlor's one, the bust of Homer's two,
The viewing room makes three, so this one here makes four.
And Mimi knows them all, and knows there are six more
With windows on each side--she'll show them all to you
The wide pine boards for sitting, and places in between.

"She wants to show you something more,/The northeast bedroom fireplace bookcase and its books."

But now she makes you follow her into the "Dark
Bedroom," a room where no light shone at all so long
Until they put the toilet in and water pipes
And sink, a bathroom now, the modern standard type.
The scent of ancient camphor (spirits, oil?) is strong
Inside the closet's drawer; it brings to mind peeled bark.

And it is dark in here, inside this "dark bedroom,"
So Mimi lights the lamp of kerosene above
The little sink--the pan behind the lamp is bright
And makes the blackest closet shadows come to light.
A door leads out the room (which Mimi gives a shove
And opens without qualms, though it could be a tomb,

So dark it is and tunnel-like in there with clothes
On hooks on either side) and then another door
Which opens once again on light: "Grandpa's study!"
Announces Mimi. In her joy her cheeks are ruddy,
She can't stand still, and Flora come! You must see more
Than those old books you're looking at, and those

Two windows filled with elms--"Come over here!" she yells
And opens up a little room, there are two more
You enter from the study, with bed and table
And microscope inside a case; *Aesop's Fables*
She's left beside the lamp beside the bed--it's for
Her visitor to see. And Mimi knows it well;

It is her favorite book: Would Flora like to read
It too? And seeing from your smile, it seems, you would,
She shows *his* microscope to you, the box of shells
Of eggs collected long ago by *him*--and now she tells
You, Flora, who her hero is, and thinks she should
Because perhaps, like you, he had a love for seeds.

And Flora see--that fireplace, tiniest of all,
Makes five we've seen so far (*she's keeping count*)--now come
To see the best part of it all! (*How can that be?*
They all appear to be the best, it seems, to Mimi.)
At study's end there is a door leads out, and from

That spot it narrows down, and winds against a wall

Until you've come up to a door again. It's hard
To open--Mimi does it with a thrust: it creaks
And swings ajar, and now the heat of Summer hits
As you descend the steps into the dark: How fits
The past of seven generations? How did it speak
To Mimi of its joys and woes in due regard

Inside the compass of that huge and treasured room?
"Shed Chamber," family called it, attic of this house
Where chests in corners stood, where duffel bags swung
Dustily from rafters and trap-door pulleys hung.
A room so wide and vast in size, you seemed a mouse,
In Summer stifling; in Winter, cold as a tomb.

("Inside the compass of that huge and treasured room?/"Shed
Chamber," attic of this house")

"Flora, watch your step! The boards are loose and so you'll
Fall right through--so follow close behind--I know the way to
Go!" (So Mimi promises us, she is stumbling
Through the dark.) There's something very still and humbling
Here, this hot and silent place she has brought you through:
Time is seated on a throne; you, on low footstool.

And there at the end of the room, dimly comes a light.
The single window's small and square, and dusty too.
But you can see enough--it takes away the gloom.
You see it's just an ordinary attic room,
With piles of books which Mimi's gone and strewn
About on rainy days. No better new delight

But drifting though the hours, looking at the barn
And butternut tree, hearing rain fall on the roof;
Or reading fashion magazines of 'Ninety Three
(Of 1893). She dreamed how that would be,
Living back then, with bustles on, and horses' hooves
Trot-trotting on the road. Fun at night was telling yarns.

You might gets bored, she thinks, and now surmises how
She'll take you down the trap-door stairs (which she so loves
For its still-working pulley system there, which when
You lift the door a little bit, it opens then
All by itself!)--and snatches up a pair of gloves
On her way down to showing you the wooden plows

Downstairs in the garage. The gloves are dainty, old
And fine, but Mimi stuffs them in her pocket, bound
To show you some new sight, the carriage house, woodpile.
She'll take them out, the gloves, to put on in a while.
Shed chamber things--a top, a bag of shells she's found
And sorted through--she likes to play with and to hold.

Downstairs beneath the long Shed Chamber room is housed
A carriage house, garage, and outhouse room--five seats,
And one of them is small--she makes you count them all;
A bench with windows spans the long ell's outer wall
Where someone's rigged a vise and left his tools. It greets
You with the dusty arms of cobwebs ill-aroused.

It's here that Mimi sits inside the square of sun
That bakes the wooden-boarded floor as it moves by,
And looks out through the window at the barn and dreams;
Or watches ant lions eat their prey--or she schemes
Of some new way to try and trick her brother, spy
On him, and follow him unseen; or shoot his bb gun.

But Mimi sees you glance around--Oh, Flora no!
Don't think you're lost, or turned around somehow, because
You can't see how to go, to get from here to there.
Yes, you must trust in her, this girl who takes you where
You'd fear to go alone--no time there ever was
When she was lost in here. She beckons--you must go.

The carriage house now holds a pile of wood; the plow
Which once the oxen pulled, will not see use again;
That old back door is hard to open--leave it shut
For now. Its granite steps have skunks beneath (*no!*) but
They're like the family now--you'll see them later when
We take the garbage out behind the barn--see how

The parents bring the little ones, and raccoons too
The same--to raid the garbage cans at night. They seem
To know they won't be harmed by anyone if they
Come near. And so it's been a hundred years--the hay's
Run through with trails they've grown accustomed to; the beams
The swallows roost upon-- it's sort of like a zoo.

And Mimi would go on and on about the birds and bees
And Blazo squirrels in the elms, and Blazo bears
Out back at night. Her mother calls them "Blazo" all,
All animals about, even those which hop and crawl,
The crickets and the frogs--"because they've lived right there
With us forever, like the Blazos, like the trees."

And Flora, how you smile! This story Mimi tells
Is true, of course, to that I'll testify. But let
Her go and lead you now--why, you're just half-way done!
The other rooms await: you won't miss even one,
Will you? Come on, I'll tell her that your heart is set
On seeing next the dining room--watch her run pell-mell!

But Mimi does not run pell-mell, but looks at me
And laughs. "Which dining room is that?" she asks,"You know
As well as I, there's two!" Of course she's right--
About the house she's rarely wrong--the old one's light
From six tall windows flows; Green Mountain's western glow
Shines on the new--both of them you'll want to see.

Where are we now? I must keep track--for talk turns one
Around; you lose where you have been. "Beside the stairs--
The trap-door stairs--and carriage house that's now a woodpile,
Remember?" Mimi asks you with a little smile
And turning points to still another door, right there
Beside the stairs--it opens on a room with sun.

It is the kitchen of the house, the oldest part,
Enhoused inside the ell, a room no longer used,
Of ample size but not so large as all the rest.
One wall is brick and rough-hewn ceiling beams attest
To its great age; against the wall a huge chartreuse
High cupboard stands alone and, empty now, apart.

("rough-hewn ceiling beams attest/ To its great age great age;")

Another stairway like the one that stands outside
The door (the one we just passed through) comes down in here;
And Mimi must tell you now, that's how she goes
When she is told she must break in the house--for those
Are times she loves the best--she *gladly* volunteers!
Her mother's lost the key again (*"Oh! We cannot get inside!"*)--

It's dropped behind the granite steps, its crack so wide
And deep it gets to keep a bunch of keys that way--
"I'll go!" she yells, delighted for the chance to be
A robber running up the woodpile stairs, you see,
Into the dark shed chamber room; she doesn't stay,
But takes the other set of stairs that goes inside

The kitchen room, and down around the dining room
And through the hall, and lets them in the door--she runs
The whole way there, such fun it is, this breaking in.
Her mother has a new key made, and so begins
The same story again. Sometimes it happens, once
Or twice, again—for it's not best to just assume

The way will not be somehow blocked--she's had to scale
The slanted roof above the cellar entrance door.
She found a toe-hold on the shingles, threw herself
Up on the roof where there the kitchen forms a shelf
And crawled in the window, and dropped onto the floor,
And raced out into the hall and grabbed the rail

("--she's had to scale/The slanted roof above the cellar entrance
door.")

And banister, and slid the whole way down the stairs--
No one there to see how she had done it--and let
Them in the door that way. Sometimes they're standing
In the sun, the loss of keys no less demanding.
She always hurries--the lone heroic one who gets
Inside the house: the rest of them, just standing there.

Oh Flora, don't encourage such disdain with smiles!
She thinks she owns the house (*but truly, does she not?*)
Because she can break in! Now let us not debate
The state of ownership just yet--it's getting late
And we have still to see, she says, an awful lot;

27

And so let's follow her and go in single file

Right past Aunt Emily's door, past the high-up bookcase
Set inside the little passage wall, pausing, stopping.
"Grandpa's Study" is overhead, Mimi tells us,
Upstairs in the ell; yet growing light compels us
All to move ahead of her to shades of sunlight dropping,
And so we find ourselves before a great fireplace

Spanning half the wall across the room. Beside it
Stands the wood-box, square; above the box, an oven
Built inside the bricks, its mantle high and wide there.
Mimi's voice is heard: "This is the biggest room where
All the windows are--there's six." And Mimi's coven
Meets in there, if such exists. She's first to deny it.

("And so we find ourselves before a great fireplace/Spanning half the wall across the room.")

She loves to come in here, the oldest dining room,
Whose windows' Indian shutters Mimi has pulled
Across until the room is dark inside as night;
And opened up again until the room is bright.
She's lain at length upon its floor's wide boards and mulled
Her mysteries in her mind and watched them rise and loom

("She's lain at length upon its floor's wide boards and mulled/Her
mysteries in her mind and watched them rise and loom")

At large against the high, high ceiling's sunny space.
She lets you stand and look around at all of it--
She's staring at a spot where used to be a sink,
When she was little, made of lead; it makes her think
Of how this "keeping room" has changed, and bit by bit
Will witness her own (*Mimi's!*) wedding taking place.

31

("...it makes her think/Of how this "keeping room" has changed,
and bit by bit/
Will witness her own (*Mimi's!*) wedding taking place")

Flora, I will go with you for now--her trances last
A good long time. She's trying to think of how rooms lie,
How sorted out they are by "common," "ours," and "theirs"
(*Have you found the dark stairway? No one goes up there!*)
Written in some will when someone way back died,
(*It's common, theirs, or ours?*)--relic-deeding from the past,

Divining of the dead. "My mother's and my room"
Her voice breaks in, "are to the right, the landing makes
A little passageway between..." Then Mimi leaps
Into the void--straight up the Dark Stairway--it's steep.
Somewhere half way up the stairs a something breaks;
And all is dust and dark and no light lights the gloom.

No need to follow--up through this, this dark stairway
Between the hall and dining room which no one climbs,

Though Mimi does it now--she's down and come around
Again to show us things we else could not have found
Out on our own: the spinning-wheel whose humming rhymes
With hummingbirds' in honeysuckle outside. Plays

Put on in this great hall (*'tis common*) or a swim
At West Pond (*running through the hall out to the porch*)
Where sun bakes dry your bathing suit and dripping hair,
Where Mimi strings the beans for supper, eating pears.
She's moving to the speed of heels still bare, bright torch
Of flashlight--fireflies flash inside a jar, then dim.

("Plays/Put on in this great hall (*'tis common*)")

("or a swim/At West Pond (*running through the hall out to the porch"*)

In this great hall are stairs built up against the wall,
The ones we climbed before, all held up by a rail.
So let us climb again, a gradual assent,
And follow it (the rail) around where it is bent
And coiled against the wall. Into that space a whale
Could fall--and yes, you'll fear that *you* could fall

If you aren't careful--Mimi always is. Around
It gathers window-seat and desk, high up and steep.
It is impossible to be oblivious
Of height up here (rather *too* adventurous
For even Mimi to stay). "Come on!" she yells, "We keep
The silver in the downstairs built-in cupboard!" (*Sounds*

Of someone in the hall at night--a robber? Creaks
Of floor-boards, someone walking...Through the secret door
We went to find each other, huddled...where's the gun?
Shhh! Don't make a sound!)...but Mimi's on the run;
We'll have to follow her and ask, to find out more.
She's gone downstairs again--it's sitting rooms she seeks.

Susan's sitting room, southeast sitting room (*warmest*
Room in all the house). In here, in Fall, September
Twenty-Eighth, in 'Sixty-Five, was born to mother
Susan, Robert Greenleaf Leavitt. These rooms by other
Names won't go: it's "Susan's Sitting Room," remember
(*Ours*), and "Emily's Sitting Room" (*theirs*). An armistice

("Susan's sitting room, southeast sitting room (*warmest*/Room in all the house")

Of war between the sisters lay, so these two rooms
Declare their names--the little vaulted ceiling hall
Between them is the one you entered early on
When first you came. The east door opens in upon
Them right and left, on both, as you walk past their walls.
And *both* will welcome *you*, dear Flora, please presume

As they both welcome Mimi in. Both have high doors
Of feathered paint protecting tiers, wide shelves of books
Or not--for they are open all the time, and volumes smell
Of dust for endless ages unexhumed; so fell
To Mimi these old treasures here--she goes to look
In them for something good to read, where bookworms bore.

37

In both a fireplace (*seven, eight!*) the book-lined sun-
Filled window seats beside each one wide-spaced.
In one the chez lounge horsehair sofa Mimi feared
To sit on for its prickly hairs (...*it felt so weird!*)
In both the golden brown of bookshelves' dusty lace
Entranced her. Both have doors out to the halls, and one

Leads to the dining room across the hall--the "new"
Let's follow, Flora, quick before she gets away!
She's sure to show us where the old dumb waiter is.
Though broken now, it's not a place she'd have us miss;
And though it doesn't move, it sometimes tends to sway.
She's pulled upon its ropes and tried to reach down to

[("Both have doors out to the halls, and one/Leads to the dining room across the hall--the "new"")]

The place where she could fix it, underneath the floor--
She longs to make it work again.   But what is this?
Instead of that, she wants to take you right outside!
I'm sure with her it's got to be a point of pride
She brings you first to see Green Mountain--can't resist
Your seeing this, which she loves best. Come out the door

("She brings you first to see Green Mountain--can't resist/Your
seeing this, which she loves best.")

That opens from the dining room, a conduit
For getting to the porch and kitchen, nothing more;
Perhaps a place for gulping down a meal, a place
You run through, if you're Mimi--there! Just see her race
Right through the dining room to open up the door
Out to the porch where all with golden sunlight's lit!

"See how it goes behind the mountain every night?"
(*It is as though she asks herself*). When she was small
She thought she'd go and look behind the mountain where
The sun would be--begged her mother take her there.
Oh Flora, see the glow of sun on leaves and sultry pall
Descending on this little world of golden light!

Screened in, the porch's marble table top is pink

With shot-through shades of blue; and cool beneath our feet,
The cement floor still holds a hint of sun-soaked noon.
But Mimi's waiting for the night, when wind and moon
Make horses out of maple limbs--they thrash and beat
Their way across the sky. She watches them and thinks.

There are two cots out here for sleeping in, and she
Sleeps every night she can in one; she hears the rain's
Torrential downpour from the porch's roof; and shakes
The covers from her in the morning when she wakes;
And leaves where it is warm, where she has lain,
And shivering, runs inside the dining room to see

If breakfast's ready yet. Her mother's burned the toast
Again and poached the eggs, and laughs (*scritch scritch, scratch
scratch*)
To see her shiver--cupboards, table, fireplace
(*That's nine*)--ahead, the kitchen's tiny cooking space.
This is the dining room, the room where plans are hatched
The gathering place the family seems to meet the most.

("This is the dining room, the room where plans are hatched/The gathering place the family seems to meet the most.")

But Mimi is the host and she won't let you stop
To ponder this. She wants to show you something else;
It's something in the kitchen, right by the cellar door.
It is the closet, something better than a store:
In here you'll find just anything--shoes, clothes, hats, belts
If you have lost it, it's in here. (*That's true! the top*

She lost--Shed Chamber top--she somehow found again
In here) and no one tries to organize it all.
Once Mimi tried, but gave it up to go outside
(A giant jumbled junk-drawer this!)--she'd rather ride
Her bike down to Sam Pease's store; or call
A friend, than fix what's perfect anyway. But when

You're ready, Flora, tired of looking at the maze
Of tangled stuff (*what's that there--a safe?*) left in
That closet there--and yes, that stove is kerosene,
The range that stands beside the little sink--I mean
To show you underneath the house. There Mimi's been
With her big brother only--cobwebs never phased

("It's something in the kitchen, right by the cellar door./It is the closet, something better than a store")

Him--*or* the spiders, *or* the damp and creepy smell--
When they went down together there to get the oil,
The kerosene, from that old tank where it was kept.
She followed him with flashlight flickering, and crept
Along behind him down the stairs, the stairs that coiled
In crooked narrowness into a sort of well

Of darkness there. Sometimes he'd open up the door
Outside, and let the sunshine in; more often not.
They'd go together cautiously--or he would stop
And scare her with a yell (*"What's that??!!!"*); or else he'd drop
His flashlight suddenly and laugh at her--he brought
Her with him just to try to scare her. There the floor

You see, was dirt, and musty-smelling like a grave
(He'd tell her this) as they went down to get the oil.
But I want you to see across the huge expanse
Of space down here, dimensions of the greater manse
That's built in underworld construction on its soil:
Each chimney base, and there are five, each vaulted cave

Of brick, each grotto like a mine conceals a trove
Of bottles, bricks and jars, and huge foundation blocks
Of granite, four feet high and wide and thick, are set
Around its huge perimeter; and light is let
Through tiny windows sunk in wells, well-boxed
Between their ends. As inlets of an ocean cove

Let in the water with the tide, so into here
The light comes floating in on shafts of sunny rays
Across the floor on sunny mornings. Then all
The cobwebbed corners light with color when it falls
On them and Mimi, when she's tiptoed there to play
Has watched the light flood in and finally lost her fear.

But where's she gone again? The ever-running sprite
Has climbed back up those crooked stairs (*be careful not*
To hit your head!)--we'll try to follow her. I'll bet
She's headed for the room you haven't been in yet
Or even seen--it's where at last she'd have you brought.
She seems to think that room's the best (*can that be right?*

She seems to think they're all the best--how can that be?)
It is the room we passed beside the window seat
The one where window panes contain the spreading elm
Outside it in the hall. This was an artist's realm
And is hers still somehow, her ghost's reclusive keep.
But Mimi doesn't know this yet; she'd have you see

Its closet, long and deep and partly filled with rolls
Of charcoal sketches, sheets of paper tied with strings
And piled or stacked against the closet wall with care.
And Mimi's whiled away the hours up in there,
Unrolled them all, seeing what each one would bring,
Whose face she'll next discover, sketched in part or whole.

Up there is where the family keeps the things that don't
Belong to us (though that will change in years to come)
It's *theirs* too, her mother's brothers, Mimi knows,
This southeast room so filled with light it almost glows.
Though Mimi's never seen an antique shop, or some
Such place where others like to store old things, she won't

Think twice if we're compelled to liken those with this,
The room we use to store these things: three buggy whips,
A tall school master's desk, a bird-cage, fans, the rare
Debris a family keeps down through the years, the layers
Piled up together in one place. *(Try not to trip*
Though, Flora, going in!) Let's go now quick--we'll miss

The happy smile she's sure to have for showing you
The last one, fireplace number *ten*. Then Flora, then--
When she has shown you all there's left to show of this
Good house and gone to bed upon the porch, and kissed
Us both good night, we'll come back to this room again,
This bedroom, artist's keep and place for storage too

And you will find it all transformed. In there will be
The spool-bed only, bookcase, writing desk. I've kept
The closet as it was in case you're up to write
An entry in your diary and want to see by light
Of wood-stove what she stored inside that crypt,
This artist of so long ago. She'd have you see

I'm sure, the sketches that she drew of him in youth,
Her cousin Robert, born like you to love all seeds
And leaves and trees. For truly, these two grew as one,
Aunt Emily's artist daughter Maude and Susan's son,
Devotee of your sacred realm. There you may read
In lines her hand has fashioned, something of that truth.

The stove I've lit against the cold that comes at night
Is lit for reasons other than necessity;
For while it warms you, you may more enjoy the way
Light blooms against the walls around the room in rays
Of beauty's deep relief and rich complexity;
No other room rewards so well the sense of sight.

And yet less said more gained; here are the keys the realm
Depends upon, dear Flora--don't lose them down the crack!
The bathroom's there (dark bedroom), there right down the hall
(*And do you hear? On cue, the whipoorwill now calls*);
The room across the hall has views the others lack.
Dutch elm disease as yet has not dared touch these elms

Which stand around this house. Green Mountain's sun's gone down.
Come rest your weary feet from travel Flora, rest
Your mythy mind and bovine tale, your soul divine,
Your restless, boundless spirit. Come and sip the wine
Of Parsonsfield. And though you like it least, it's best
You sleep--Old Joe will wake you going into town

The first thing in the morning; at the crack of dawn.
Then Mimi will be up. Then will you give us news
From Cambridge, Troy, and Rome? It's written night and day
Are all the same to her who rows for Rome--she may
Have found (our Julia may), the long-sought sea-shelled clue
She's walked that beach so long to fix her gaze upon:

You'd be the first to know. So Flora, stay the night
And rest in peace, and in that window from the east
Will come the sun and strike you while you sleep; the birds
Will sing perhaps the sweetest songs you've ever heard
And you'll not want to leave your bed. What better feast
Of paradise than sounds of birds and morning light?

Though not a Cambridge (Mimi's been there too), nor home,
This house enshrined with elms and rustling maple trees
Invites you in to share with others of your kind,
A Rome away from Rome, a respite for your mind.
That Julia visit next, I see, is Mimi's urgent plea.
(It is her right to ask, for this is Mimi's home.)

(*Flora is the protagonist of Julia Budenz's *The Gardens of Flora
Baum*, an epic poem in five books, published by Carpathian Press.
For more information about Julia Budenz go to:
http://www.carpathiapress.com.)

PROFESSIONAL BOOKS FROM THE BLAZO-LEAVITT HOUSE

Inventory and provenance as compiled by Mary Freeman
(mimi.freeman@gmail.com)

INTRODUCTION

The professional library of the Blazo-Leavitt house is a collection of books belonging to Robert Tibbetts Blazo (**RTB**), his two sons-in-law Howard Hiram Browne (**HHB**) and John Greenleaf Leavitt (**JGL**), and his grandson Robert Greenleaf Leavitt (**RGL**). The majority are law books, the remainder being those used by their owners in their professions of medicine, religion, and education; additionally, encyclopedias, dictionaries and reference books are included. All were collected and kept in the Blazo homestead in North Parsonsfield until 1973 when the house was sold, but have remained with the family ever since. The Blazo-Leavitt house is listed on the National Register of Historic Places.

In the following inventory, books **signed** by their owners **ROBERT TIBBETTS BLAZO** (lawyer, educator), **HOWARD HIRAM BROWNE** (lawyer, doctor, poet), **JOHN GREELEAF LEAVITT** (minister), and **ROBERT GREENLEAF LEAVITT** (botanist) are accompanied by their **initials in bold lettering** as follows: **RTB, JGL, HHB, and RGL**.

Included in the collection is **THE WHITE HILLS**, by Cornelius Weygandt, Henry Holt and Co. New York: 1933. It has a chapter entitled "Love and the Law Long ago," that chronicles the diary and love letters between the young lawyer **RTB** and his bride to be Mary (Polly) Freeman (1812-1890). In its margins are inscriptions by **RGL**, his grandson. Letters by the author are included in the botany books collection; additionally, a diploma conferring a medical degree (in fine condition) belonging to the doctor is part of the collection too.

LAW

The law books in this collection belonged to **Robert Tibbetts Blazo** (1797-18900 and his son-in-law **Howard Hiram Browne** . The signature of the latter is invariably accompanied by the inscribed Latin motto "*Palmam qui meruit ferat*," which translates to "Let he who merits the palm possess it." In other words, "If you wish to gain recognition, work hard for it."

(SETS)

1. CRUISE ON REAL PROPERTY, William Cruise, First American Edition, New York: printed for Alsop, Brannon, and Alsop, City Hotel, Broadway, **1808**. (Five volumes) **BOX 2**

2. KENT'S COMMENTARIES, COMMENTARIES ON AMERICAN LAW, Tenth Edition, Boston: Little, Brown and Co., **1860**. (Three volumes) **BOX 4 HHB**

3. GREENLEAF ON EVIDENCE, A TREATISE ON LAW OF EVIDENCE, Simon Greenleaf. Tenth Edition. Boston: Little, Brown and Co., Riverside, Cambridge, **1858**. (Three volumes: 1,2, and 3).
BOX 2 HHB

4. PHILIPS ON EVIDENCE, TREATISE ON THE LAW OF EVIDENCE. New York: Gould and Banks, State St., Albany, **1823**. (Two volumes)
BOX 4

5. SELWYN'S *NISI PRIUS*, APRIDGEMENT OF THE LAW OF *NISI PRIUS*. Philadelphia: William P. Ferrand, **1807, 1808**. (Three volumes: 1, 2, and 3).
BOX 6

6. HEARD'S LAW, HEARD ON CRIMINAL LAW, Franklin Fiske Heard. Second Edition, revised for Mass. and other states with full precedents. Boston: Little, Brown, and Company. **1882**. (One volume)
BOX 6 HHB

7. HEARD'S PRECEDENTS OF EQUITY PLEADING. Boston: Little, Brown, and Company. **1884**. (One volume).
BOX 6 HHB

8. PARSONS ON CONTRACTS, Fourth Edition. Theophilis Parsons, Professor of Law, Harvard. Boston: Little, Brown, and Company. **1860**. (Two volumes) **BOX 6 HHB**

9. SHARSWORDS'S BLACKSTONE'S COMMENTARIES, COMMENTARIES ON THE LAWS OF ENGLAND IN FOUR BOOKS BY WILLIAM BLACKSTONE. George Sharswood, Professor of Institute of Law in the University of

Pennsylvania. In two volumes. Philadelphia: Child and
Peterson. **1860.** (Two volumes)
BOX 10 HHB

**10. WASHBURN ON REAL PROPERTY, TREATISE ON
THE AMERICAN LAW OF REAL PROPERTY.** Emory
Washburn, Second Edition. Boston: Little, Brown and
Company. **1864.** (One volume)
BOX 8 HHB

**11. HILLIARD'S ABRIDGEMENT, AN ABRIDGEMENT
OF THE AMERICAN LAW OF REAL PROPERTY.** Francis
Hilliard. Boston: Charles C. Little and James Brown. Volumes
one and two. **1838.** (Two volumes)
BOX 8 HHB

**12. HILLIARDS ON SALES, THE LAW OF SALES ON
PERSONAL PROPERTY.** Francis Hilliard. Second edition.
Philadelphia: T. & J. W. Johnson and & Co. **1860.** (One
volume)
BOX 8

13. HILLIARDS ON TORTS OR PRIVATE WRONGS.
Francis Hilliard. Second edition. Volume I and Volume II.
Boston: Little, Brown, and Company. **1861** (Two volumes)
BOX 5 HHB

**14. HILLIARD'S ELEMENTS OF LAW, ELEMENTS OF
LAW BEING A COMPREHENSIVE SUMMARY OF
AMERICAN CIVIL JURISPRUDENCE.** Francis Hilliard.
Boston: Hilliard, Gray, and Company. **1835** (One volume)
BOX 8

15. DIGEST OF MASSACHUSETTS REPORTS. A DIGEST OF THE CASES ARGUED AND DETERMINED IN THE SUPREME JUDICIAL COURT OF THE COMMONWEALTH OF MASSACHUSETTS FROM SEPTEMBER 1804 TO NOVEMBER 1815. Lewis Bigelow. Cambridge: University Press, Hilliard and Metcalf. **1818**. (One volume)
BOX 1 RTB

16. MASSACHUSETTS DIGEST, BEING A DIGEST OF THE DECISIONS OF THE SUPREME JUDICIAL COURT OF MASSACHSETTS; BENNET & HEGRD, BEING A DIGEST OF THE DECISCONS OF THE MASSACHUSETTS SUPREME JUDICIAL COURT OF MASSACHUSETTS, 1804-1857. Volume I: A-H; Volume II: I-W. (Two volumes)
BOX 11 RTB & HHB

17. THE REVISED STATUTES OF THE STATE OF MAINE, Portland, Bailey & Noyes, **1871** (One volume)
BOX 7

(SINGLE VOLUMES)
1. STORY ON PROMISSORY NOTES. Joseph Story, Fifth edition. Boston: Little, Brown, and Company. **1859**.
BOX 10 HHB

2. MASON'S PRACTICE, NEW ENGLAND STATES. THE PRACTICE OF CIVIL ACTIONS. Joseph Mason. First edition. Boston: Little, Brown and Company. **1880**.
BOX 9 HHB

3. OLIVER'S CONVEYANCING, PRACTICAL CONVEYANCING. Benjamin Oliver. Hallowell: Masters, Smith, and Company. **1853.**
BOX 10 HHB

4. LAWRENCE'S WHEATON ON INTERNATIONAL LAW, ELEMENTS OF INTERNATIONAL LAW. Henry Wheaton. Second Annotated Edition. William Beach Lawrence. Boston: Little, Brown and Company. **1855.** London: Sampson Low, Son and Company. **1863.**
BOX 7

5. NOY'S MAXIMS. INCLUDING PREFACES TO EARLIER EDITION BY WILLIAM WALLER HENING, RICHMOND, W.M. BLITHERWOOD, ESQ. OF LINCOLN'S INN, CHARLES BARTON, INNER TEMPLE, ESQ. , AN ANALYSIS OF THE LAWS OF ENGLAND. MAXIMS IN LAW AND EQUITY, SECOND AMERICAN EDITION. 1824.
BOX 5 RTB

6. CHITTY ON CONTRACTS, A TREATISE ON THE LAW OF CONTRACTS. THE SIXTH ENGLISH EDITION. JOHN RUSSELL. Tenth American Edition. Springfield: G. and C. Merriam. **1860.**
BOX 9 HHB

7. LAWES ON PLEADING, A TREATISE ON PLEADING IN CIVIL ACTIONS. Edward Lawes of the Inner Temple. First American from the First London edition. Portsmouth, N.H.: Thomas and Tappan. **1808.**
BOX 9 HHB

8. WILLS ON CIRCUMSTANCE--EVIDENCE, AN ESSAY ON THE PRINCIPLES OF CIRCUMSTANCIAL EVIDENCE. William Wills, Esq. From the Third London edition. Philadelphia: T. and J. W. Johnson and Co. **1857.**
BOX 9 HHB

9. HAMMOND'S *NISI PRIUS*, A TREATISE ON *NISI PRIUS*. Anthony Hammond, Esq. of the Inner Temple. First American from the last American edition. Exeter, N.H.: George Lamson. **1823**.
BOX 9 RTB

10. STEVEN ON PLEADING, A TREATISE ON PLEADING IN CIVIL ACTIONS. Henry John Steven. Fourth American Edition. Philadelphia: R. H. Small. **1841.**
BOX 9 RTB

11. COLBY'S PRACTICE, THE PRACTICE IN CIVIL ACTIONS AND PROCEEDINGS AT LAW IN MASSACHSETTS. Boston: Charles C. Little and James Brown. **1848.**
BOX 5

12. LAWYER'S RECORD AND OFFICIAL REGISTER OF THE UNITED STATES. Charles Ulman. New York: Barnes and Co., 1872.
BOX 10
13. THE STATESMAN or PRINCIPLES OF LEGISLATION AND LAW. John Holmes. Augusta: Severance and Dorr.
BOX 6 HHB

MEDICINE

1. GRIFFETH'S UNIVERSAL FORMULARY. R. Eglesfeld
Griffeth, M.D. Philadelphia: Lea and Blanchard. **1850.**
BOX 8 HHB

**2. DEWEES ON CHILDREN, TREATISE ON THE
PHYSICAL AND MEDICAL TREATMENT OF
CHILDREN.** William Dewees, M.D. Ninth Edition.
Philadelphia: Lea & Blanchard. **1847.**
BOX 8 HHB

**3. PAINE'S PRACTICE OF MEDICINE, A TREATISE ON
THE PRICIPLES AND PRACTICE OF MEDICINE AND
PATHOLOGY, DISEASES OF WOMEN AND CHILDREN.**
W. Paine, M.D. Second edition. Philadelphia: University
Publishing Society, **1866.**
BOX 3 HHB

DIVINITY

**1. PALEY'S WORKS, THE WORKS OF WILLIAM PALEY,
D.D., COMPLETE IN ONE VOLUME.** Philadelphia: J.J.
Woodward. **1831.** 604 p.
BOX 1 JGL

2. SCOTT'S BIBLE, VOL II, RUTH-ESTHER. Thomas Scott.
Exeter, N.H.: Samuel Armstrong and Crocker and Brewster.
New York: J. P. Haven **(n.d. but signature dated "June 5th,
1827")** (One volume) **BOX 1 RTB**

3. SCOTT'S BIBLE, VOL.V, MATT-ACTS, Thomas Scott.
Exeter, N.H.: Andrew Poor and James Derby. **1830.**
BOX 1 RTB

4. HOLY BIBLE. New York: American Bible Society, instituted in MDCCCXVI. **1853. BOX 3 RTB**

5. HOLY BIBLE. New York: American Bible Society, instituted in MDCCCXVI. **1867. BOX 3 RTB** (missing spine cover)

DICTIONARIES, DIRECTORIES, ENCYCLOPEDIAS, AND LEXICONS

1. JOHNSON AND WALKER'S ENGLISH DICTIONARY, JOHNSON AND WALKER'S ENGLISH DICTIONARY COMBINED, AS IMPROVED BY TODD AND ABRIDGED BY CHAL; WITH WALKER'S PRONOUCING DICTIONARY, TO WHICH IS ADDED WALKER'S KEY TO THE CLASSICAL PRONUNCIATION OF GREEK, LATIN, AND SCRIPTURE PROPER NAMES. Boston: Charles Ewer and T. Harrington Carter. 1156 p. **1828.** Fine.

2. LEVERETT'S LEXICON OF THE LATIN LANGUAGE, A NEW AND COPIOUS LEXICON OF THE LATIN LANGUAGE. F.P. Leverett. Boston: Bazin & Ellsworth. **1850. BOX 1 JGL**

3. NEW AMERICAN CYCLOPEDIA (ALL VOLUMES). NEW YORK: D. APPLETON& COMPANY, SOUTHERN DISTRICT OF NEW YORK. 1857. BOXES 12, 13 AND 14. HHB

4. LIPPENCOTT'S UNIVERSAL PRONOUNCING DICTIONARY OF BIOGRAPHY AND MYTHOLOGY. J. Thomas. Philadelphia: J.B. Lippencott and Co., **1871. BOX 5**

ORATION

1. ORATIONS AND SPEECHES, ORATIONS AND SPEECHES ON VARIOUS OCCASIONS. Edward Everett. Boston: Little, Brown and Company. **1860.** (Volume I, 1860: Sixth Edition. Volume II, 1860: Sixth Edition. Volume III, 1959.) **BOX 4 HHB**

NATURAL PHILOSOPHY AND BOTANY

1. A SYSTEM OF NATURAL PHILOSOPHY, J.L. Comstock, M.D., New York: Pratt, Woodford and Co., 1849. **BOX 1 RTB**

2. OUTLINES OF BOTANY, Robert Greenleaf Leavitt, American Book Company, **1901**. Copyright The president and Fellows of Harvard College. With associated notes and letters by the author explaining the origin of the book. Signatures by author's wife and daughter IGL and CLH. **BOX 15 RGL.**

3. OUTLINES OF BOTANY WITH FLORA, Robert Greenleaf Leavitt, American Book Co., 1901 Copyright The president and Fellows of Harvard College. With associated notes and letters by the author explaining the origin of the book, and a 1903 letter from Cuba to his father in law by the author describing his collection of orchids, is included. **BOX 15 RGL.**

4. THE FOREST TREES OF NEW ENGLAND, Robert Greenleaf Leavitt, The Arnold Arboretum of Harvard University, **1933**. With associated newspaper articles reviewing the book, pamphlets announcing its publication, and notes and letters by the author explaining its origin. Photograph of **RGL** collecting specimens is included. **BOX 15, RGL**

5. THE MAINE WOODS, Henry David Thoreau, James Osgood and Co., Boston: 1871. Signed by Susan Chapman Blazo Leavitt with inscription by **RGL** as to its influence on him. **BOX 15 RGL**

6. **THE WHITE HILLS**, by Cornelius Weygandt, Henry Holt and Co. New York: 1933. It has a chapter entitled "Love and the Law Long ago," that chronicles the diary and love letters between the young lawyer **RTB** and his bride to be Mary (Polly) Freeman (1812-1890). In its margins are inscriptions by **RGL**, his grandson. **BOX 15 RGL**

REPORTS AND REGISTRIES

1. **LOWELL CITY DOCUMENTS.** Lowell, Mass: *VOX Populi* Press, City Printers, **1885**. (fine)
BOX 7 HHB

2. **THE LOWELL DIRECTORY, 1886. STREET DIRECTORY, BUSINESS DIRECTORY.** Sampson Murdock & Co. (formerly Sampson, Davenport, and Co. Lowell, Mass: Joshua Merrill & Son. (fine) **BOX 3 HHB**

3. **BOYER'S LEGAL DIRECTORY,** Joseph Boyer, Philadelphia, PA 1887. (fine)
BOX 3 HHB

US GOVERNMENT PUBLICATIONS

1. **PERRY'S EXPLORATION INTO JAPAN Narrative of an American Squadron to the China Seas for the Years 1852, 1853, and 1854 under command of Commodore Perry, US Navy. Published by order of the Congress of the United States. 1856. Washington AOP, Printer: Nicholson** Spine cover attached but loose. Color fold-out lithographs. (Nude bathing scene included in this edition.) **BOX 11 JGL**

PROVENANCE

Howard Hiram Browne (HHB) Lawyer, Doctor, Poet
(1838-1897)

Born: Cornish, Maine, Nov.15, 1838.

From *Local and National Poets of America with Interesting Biographical Sketches and Choice Selections from Over One Thousand Living American Poets* by Thomas William Herringshaw, Amer. Pub. Association, 1892, we learn: "After teaching School for a while, Mr. Browne studied law and was admitted to the bar in 1962. Four years later he was married Emily M. Blazo. Mr. Browne now resides in Boston with his wife and daughter. Since his youth Mr. Browne has been an occasional contributor of both verse and prose to various literary and other publications." He practiced law first in Limerick, Maine and then for years in Lowell, Massachusetts.

John Greenleaf Leavitt (JGL) ((1834–1885) Educator, Minister

An early student at Parsonsfield Seminary at Parsonsfield, Maine, he returned to his alma mater in 1859 to serve as the school's principal for one year. He married Susan Chapman Blazo, daughter of one of the Seminary's co-founders, Robert Tibbetts Blazo. Rev. J. Greenleaf Leavitt was father of Robert Greenleaf Leavitt and later spent his life as a Congregationalist minister at Webster, Massachusetts.

Robert Tibbetts Blazo (RTB) York County Maine Lawyer (1797-1890)

The following biography is written by **Howard Hiram Browne, RTB's** son-in-law.)

Robert Tibbets Blazo was born in North Parsonsfield, York county, Maine, Aug. 11, 1797, and died at that place May 25, 1890, ninety-two years, nine months and fourteen days. The name is of French origin, and not a common one in this country. Indeed, all who bear the name in New England, at the present time, are believed to be descendants from William Blazo, or Blaso as originally spelled, who came from France, tradition says from Bordeaux, to Newcastle or Greenland, N.H., early ion the eighteenth century. It is stated in the alleged History of Parsonsfield, that he came over in the year 1735. That he came to this country much earlier than that is proved by the fact that in 1727 he is mentioned in the New Hampshire Provincial Records as one of the first settlers of Epson, who migrated from New Castle and Greenland where they had previously settled. According to the ancient annals of Epson, "the town had been settled more than thirty years before the father of a family died there, and the first man buried in the oldest graveyard (that by the meeting house)) was William Blaso." The date of his death is not given, but it appears he was living as late as 1760, for him that year he, with others of his townsmen, signed a petition to governor Wentworth.

It is not known whether he married before or after coming from France--nothing of his wife save that her name was Catherine, and that, according to the accords of the First Church in Greenland, she "owned ye covenants" in 1728. This being after their removal to Epson, it is probable that, being without a church or minister in the new settlement, they continued their connection with the church at Greenland. This is evident, too, from the fact that the baptism of their children are recorded there for several years after. These are, Amos, Dec, 72--; Judith, 1728; John, 1734; Jonathan, 1734; Thomas, 1737; Sarah, 1745; Mehitable, Apr. 30, 1749--There was also a Paul, who birth or baptism is not given, who enlisted in the continental Army, Dec. 10, 1782, as did Thomas, three days later.

Although the year in which Amos Blazo was born is not given he was, probably, the oldest of the children. November 2, 1761, he was married to Joanna Libby, born, Oct. 16, 1737, daughter of Isaac and Mary Libby, of Rye, N. H., and a lineal descendant of John Libby who came from England to Scarborough, Maine in 1630. His residence, as given at that time, was Chichester. The following year, and again in 1766, he and his brother John signed petitions as residents of Epson.

At some time previous to March, 1778, he removed to Parsonsfield, (then called Parson's Town) Maine. He with others, at that time, petitioned, as inhabitants of that place, for a road to Wakefield. There he permanently settled upon the land that has ever since remained in the possession of his descendants.

The children of Amos and Joanna (Libby) Blazo, were: Catherine, born, August 11, 1762—died, Dec.16, 1809; Daniel, born, Sept 1764--died, January 19, 1802; John, born Dec. 4, 1766--died, Nov. 4, 1821; Joseph, born June 16, 1768--died, June 1827; Ebeneezer, born, 1770; Jonathan, born, 1775, died, June, 1817; William, born, March 1, 1777--died, August 25, 1830; Polly, born Apr. 2, 1779--died, Oct. 18, 17--.

Amos Blazo died, Feb. 23, 1821. His wife died, Aug, 30, 1810. Daniel Blazo, above named, married Abigail Chapman, daughter of Job and Penelope (Philbrook) Chapman, and a lineal descendant, in the fifth generation, of Edward Chapman who came from England to Ipswich, Mass., in 1636. She died, Oct. 13, 1842. John Blazo, the youngest son of Daniel and Abigail (Chapman) Blazo, born, Nov. 1799, resided in Parsonsfield until his decease, in 1878. The oldest son, Robert Tibbets Blazo, the subject of this sketch, remained in his native town during his early boyhood, attending the common schools. He afterwards attended the well known academy at Limerick, Fryeburgh, and Waldoborough N.H. Subsequently he was engaged in teaching at Sandwich, N.H.; having among his pupils the, afterwards, Rev. Hosea Quimby, the late Hon. John Wentworth, of Chicago, and Harrison and Albert Hoyt, the former a well known Episcopal clergyman, the latter an artist of much celebrity.

Having studied law, in the offices of Ira Q. Bean, Esp., of Sandwich, and Samuel Emerson Esq. of Moultonborough, he was admitted to practice at the New Hampshire bar, in 1830. He commenced practice at Moultonborough where he remained about four years, then removed to Sandwich. Mr. Blazo married, Dec. 24, 1835, Mary Freeman, daughter of James Otis Freeman, a most estimable lady who survives him. They had four children, two sons and two daughters, all of whom are now living.

In 1839 he relinquished his law practice at Sandwich and removed to his native town where he afterwards resided, on the old family homestead, until his decease. During the later years of his life he was principally engaged in farming and other business interests, taking little or no active part in the practice of his profession. Though always taking a deep interest in all public affairs, Mr. Blazo never sought nor accepted any office or political preferment other than such as belonged to his own town.

In educational matters he felt a deep interest, and took an active part in the establishment and maintenance of the North Parsonsfield Seminary, the first ever established by the Freewill Baptist denomination, and of which he was, for many years, treasurer and member of the board of trustees.

Mr. Blazo was a man of kindly nature; in his habits quiet and retiring; in his living temperate and abstemious. He possessed a scholarly mind, was fond of books, and was an assiduous reader of them, even up to the closing days of his life. In thought and in the conduct of business affairs he was conservative and cautious. He possessed a marked individuality, a strong will, and had the courage of his convictions. In the course of his protracted life these characteristics have made him well and widely known, and he should long be remembered as a kind friend, a good citizen and an honest man.

Robert Greenleaf Leavitt (RGL) Professor of Botany, Harvard; head of Biology Department at New Jersey College (then known as New Jersey State Teacher's College); research scientist, contributor to the Smithsonian, and author. (1865-1942)

Dr. Leavitt was born in Parsonsfield, Maine. His parents were Susan Chapman Blazo and John Greenleaf Leavitt, a Congregational minister, who had been married in the early 1860s.[1] He was an early botany professor at Harvard College, where he had graduated in the class of 1889 after attending Worcester Academy.[2] Then went to Harvard College, living in Cambridge. While there he went in for athletics and became intercollegiate pole vault champion as well as a prize-winning jumper.[1] He was graduated AB in June 1889. He taught school at DeVeaux School in Niagara Falls, N.Y., then at Williston Seminary in Easthampton, Mass. Following his Harvard education, Leavitt began publishing widely in the field of botany, including articles in *The American Naturalist*, *The Botanical Gazette*, *Science* magazine (the official publication of the American Association for the Advancement of Science), the Boston Society of Natural

History magazine as well as other publications in the field. In 1899 Leavitt was named assistant professor at Harvard.[3]

Leavitt subsequently earned his Doctor of Philosophy in biology at Harvard in 1904.[4] He wrote *Leavitt's Outlines of Botany,* a standard text book at the time; it was published by the Harvard University Press.[1] Leavitt spent some nine years at the Ames Botanical Laboratory in study, research, writing and collecting specimens, including trips to Cuba and Europe. Following his time at the Ames Botanical Laboratory, Leavitt became a high school botany teacher in Massachusetts and later in New Jersey. "College teaching is the least interesting," Leavitt wrote his Harvard classmates, "normal school the most interesting."

As the head of the biological department of the New Jersey Normal and Model Schools, Dr. Leavitt served as a high school teacher in Trenton, New Jersey, as well as overseeing statewide efforts to teach botany and the natural sciences.

"I expect to put in the rest of my time before I retire to my farm in Maine in helping to improve the schools of this State System," Leavitt wrote to his Harvard class. "At

60 I expect to retire for 40 years of research, with special reference to fruits adaptable to Maine, at my experiment station in a beautiful country among the foothills of the White Mountains. (My great, great grandfather was a man of God-given taste in scenery)."[5]

In the following years, Leavitt authored many textbooks in the field of botany, many for high school students, including his *Outlines of Botany for the High School Laboratory and Classroom*, which was widely reprinted.

Robert Greenleaf Leavitt was the son of John Greenleaf Leavitt, an early student at Parsonsfield Seminary[6] at Parsonsfield, Maine, who returned to his alma mater in 1861 to serve as the school's principal for one year, when he married Susan C. Blazo, daughter of one of the Seminary's co-founders. (Dr. Leavitt served as a trustee for the Parsonsfield Seminary.[7]) Rev. J. Greenleaf Leavitt later spent his life as a Congregationalist minister at Webster, Massachusetts.[8] The home built by his wife's Blazo ancestors descended in the family of Rev. Greenleaf Leavitt. (The Blazo-Leavitt House is listed on the National Register of Historic Places.)

DR. ROBERT G. LEAVITT

Dr. Robert Greenleaf Leavitt

Dr. Leavitt married Ida Gertrude (Ruggli) Leavitt, a 1901 graduate of Radcliffe College, at Arlington, Massachusetts in 1906, following the death of his first wife Janet (Shumway).[9] Robert Greenleaf Leavitt and his first wife had two sons, Robert and Russell, both of whom attended Harvard College. Dr. Leavitt and his second wife Ida Ruggli had two daughters, Rosamund, who died in infancy, and Constance. Following his service as a high school teacher in New Jersey, Robert Greenleaf Leavitt retired to his farm in Maine, where he raised 40 varieties of apples. (From Wikipedia)

Photograph of the Blazo-Leavitt house circa 1915

Blazo-Leavitt House From Wikipedia

The Blazo-Leavitt House is a large two-story white-clapboard mansion [1] built in Parsonsfield, Maine, in 1812 by William Blazo, uncle to prominent Parsonsfield lawyer Robert Tibbetts Blazo. Oral tradition holds that Robert T. Blazo, as a young man of fifteen in 1812, and later aged twenty in 1817, had helped with the construction of his uncle's house. This story seems credible because Robert had been bound out to his uncle William when Robert's father (William's brother) Daniel

Blazo fell from a beam at a barn-raising in and broke his neck, dying in 1802. Later, ownership of the house passed to the nephew, Robert T. Blazo. The house next was passed on to Robert Blazo's two daughters, Susan Blazo Leavitt and Emily Blazo Browne. Emily's daughter Maude Browne left no descendants, and the house eventually passed into the hands of Susan Blazo Leavitt's son, Robert Greenleaf Leavitt, his wife Ida Ruggli Leavitt, and his three children Russell Greenleaf Leavitt, Robert Keith Leavitt, and Constance Ruggli Leavitt Hanson. Thus it is called the Blazo-Leavitt house. The house is on the National Register of Historic Places.

The Blazo-Leavitt house has five large brick chimneys. The house also boasts elaborately carved and pillared entrances with leaded glass fans and sidelights, paneled doors, and small-paned windows. The main Ell of the home was built in 1812, the main part of house being constructed five years later in 1817. William Blazo was son of Amos Blazo, who in turn was son of William Blazo of Bordeaux, France, who immigrated to America sometimes before 1727, settling first in Greenland, New Hampshire, and later in Epson. Amos Blazo is recorded in the History of Parsonsfield as having been North

Parsonsfield's first settler, clearing the fields at "Blazo's Corner" in March of 1778. [2] Amos Blazo had five sons, four of whom settled on nearby farms. It was Amos's son William who built the Blazo House, later selling it to his nephew, and Amos's grandson, Robert Tibbetts Blazo.

Robert Tibbetts Blazo had begun his career as a schoolmaster. One of his pupils was fifteen year old Mary Freeman of Sandwich, New Hampshire who would become his bride eight years later [3] Before the marriage Robert Blazo practiced law for a time in Moultonborough, New Hampshire, but eventually the couple settled in Parsonsfield where Blazo practiced law, and was for many decades Justice of the Peace and Post Master. The couple had four children: Susan, Daniel, Charles and Emily. Descendants of Daniel still reside in the Daniel Blazo house directly across from the Blazo-Leavitt house at Blazo's Corner.

All four Blazo children attended Parsonsfield Seminary, to which their father had conveyed the land and helped establish. Here Susan Blazo met John Greenfield Leavitt, a fellow student from Buckfield, Maine, who had come to Parsonfield to prepare for Waterville College (today's Colby College). The couple married, and moved into the Blazo house with her parents; they had one child, Robert Greenleaf Leavitt.[4] Emily Blazo married Howard Hiram Browne, and they too took up residence in the house; they had one child, Maude Browne, who later became a portrait artist. Because Maude Browne was unable to have children, eventually ownership of the house came to the Leavitts and to their son Robert Greenleaf Leavitt, a well-known Harvard-educated botanist and educator. After Robert G. Leavitt's death in 1942, Robert's wife Ida and their children, and grandchildren, and great grandchildren, continued living in it every summer. Robert Greenleaf Leavitt's daughter, Constance Leavitt Hanson, with great regret, sold the house in 1973. Parsonsfield Seminary, Parsonsfield, Maine. Robert Tibbetts Blazo, second owner of the Blazo-Leavitt House, conveyed land on which Seminary was built and helped found the Seminary.

The Blazo-Leavitt house faces south, and its western side faces Green Mountain, part of the Sandwich Mountains of New Hampshire, the foothills of the White Mountains. Nearby is the Leavitt Plantation Forest (connected with another branch of the Leavitt family), an 8,603-acre tract that is the largest contiguous block of forestland south of Sebago Lake, Maine. Leavitt Plantation Forest covers 20 percent of Parsonsfield's land. The tract of forest land is now under permanent conservation easement, thanks to its purchase by the State of Maine and the Nature Conservancy, which purchased the entire parcel to prevent its development.

(**From** *Maine's Historic Places,* by Beard and Smith, Downeast Books, 1982, p. 389: Blazo-Leavitt House, Route 160--1812-17): "This expansive high-style federal homestead reflects both externally and internally an advanced level of woodworking technique. It is believed that the exceptional woodwork was the work of ship's carpenters from Portsmouth who were left unemployed."

RESIDENTS OF THE HOUSE, 1812-1973

William Blazo Mar 1, 1777—Aug 25, 1830

Mehitable Wedgewood Blazo May 10, 1786—July 24, 1862

Robert Tibbetts Blazo Aug. 11, 1797—May 24, 1890

Mary (Polly) Freeman Blazo Aug 1, 1812—Aug. 22, 1900

Susan French Freeman Cooke May 22, 1783—August 22, 1844

Lott Cooke (stepfather of Mary (Polly) Freeman Blazo)

Daniel Otis Freeman Blazo Nov. 6, 1836—Aug. 22, 1914

Susan Chapman Blazo Leavitt Feb. 14, 1839—Feb. 13, 1920

John Greenleaf Leavitt Aug. 13, 1834--1885

Charles Blazo Aug. 3, 1842—Oct. 20, 1926

Emily Maria Blazo Browne Nov. 22, 1844—Oct. 19, 1924

Howard Hiram Browne, 1838--1897

Maude Browne June 7, 1867—Dec.4, 1932

Robert Greenleaf Leavitt Sept. 28, 1865—Oct. 2, 1942

Ella Janet Shumway Leavitt 1865—Feb 17, 1902

Robert Keith Leavitt Aug. 20, 1895—May, 1967

Russell Greenleaf Leavitt Dec. 19, 1896—Jan, 1984

Ida Gertrude Ruggli Leavitt, Oct. 8, 1872—July 1, 1958

Constance Ruggli Leavitt Hanson, Dec. 19, 1907—April 8, 1998

Hodge Jackson Hanson Oct, 1904-1997

Robert Jackson Hanson Dec. 3, 1936—Dec 16, 2011

Mary Freeman Hanson (aka Mimi Hanson) Nov. 11, 1943—

Ralph Bruce Wentworth, Aug. 1, 1936--2018

Eve Ruggli Wentworth July 23, 1963—

Rachael Chapman Wentworth Eastman, Oct. 9, 1965—

Donna Freeman Wentworth, Sept. 14, 1969—

Erika Hanson Wentworth Sept. 14, 1969—

Robert Tibbetts Blazo

This photograph is of a charcoal portrait by his granddaughter **Maude Browne, a professional portrait artist**. She was the only child of Howard Hiram Browne (**HHB**) and Emily Blazo Browne, granddaughter of Robert Tibbetts Blazo.

***Amos Blazo, from records compiled by Robert Tibbetts Blazo
(RTB), grandson***

Amos Blazo was out in the old French war in 1755–6. When he
lived in Epson, he was neighbor to Mayor McClary who was killed
at the Battle of Bunker Hill. Amos was a great _____ and
could walk sixty miles in a day. He also was a disciple of Isaac
Walton, a great fisherman. There is a place in the River in Epson,
N.H. where he fished, which is called Blazo Hole. In the old
French war he crossed Lake George with the army that occupied
one hundred and twenty batteries. He was a natural singer, fond of
voice music and an honest upright man. Although not a professed
Christian, all the _____ preachers who chose found a
welcome resting hour at his house.

***Article about Robert Greenleaf Leavitt from the Lewiston Journal
Illustrated Magazine Section, Saturday, August 7, 1937,
Magazine Section A--40.***

Maine Author Writes Books at Request of Harvard College: "Forest
Trees of New England", Handbook of Arnold Arboretum, the
Latest, Lives in Fine Ancestral Home, North Parsonsfield
By Mary Carpenter Kelley

On an elm-shaded corner near the seminary in the beautiful
upland village of North Parsonsfield, York County, stands an

imposing white house. Its square frame of generous size and good proportions, its five great chimneys, its exquisitely carved and pillared entrances with their leaded glass fans and sidelights, its paneled doors, its small paned windows and its long ell with arched sheds mark it as of that period when wealth and good taste combined to produce the best in colonial architecture.

It is the mansion built by William Blazo early in the nineteenth century and now occupied by his brother Daniel's great-grandson, Dr. Robert Greeenleaf Leavitt of Morrisville, Pennsylvania, and Washington, D.C.

Dr. Leavitt was born in that mansion in the very room on the front corner of the first floor in which he told me the other day about his family, his work and the many worthwhile accomplishments of a long, busy life. **Perhaps the two things for which he is best known are the books written at the request of Harvard College, a revision of Asa Gray's Lessons in Botany called "Outlines of Botany," and in 1933, "The Forest Trees of New England" to be used as a handbook for the Arnold Arboretum.** The latter is a volume of fifty-one short chapters with descriptions of all the native New England trees, many introduced trees, and illustrations of the leaves of the deciduous trees and of the conifers. It has been printed inn a special edition on permanent paper and has been placed in the Widener Library at Harvard, the Congressional Library in Washington in Washington, the Piermont Morgan Library for Classics in New York City, in the British Museum and in many other important libraries besides.

It was the noted Dr. George Lincoln Goodale (born in Saco, by the way), for many years head of the Department of Botany at Harvard, who first asked Dr. Leavitt to revise Gray's Lessons in Botany. This was while Dr. Leavitt was acting as director of summer courses in botany. For nine years previous to 1908 he was assistant with Professor Oakes Ames of Harvard, the greatest orchidologist in the world, and worked in the Ames private research laboratory in North Easton. During this period he wrote the National Herbarium in Washington, which was receiving the government collections of orchids, that the Ames laboratory was the place where they could best be studied, and from then on the orchids were sent to North Easton. While working with them, Dr. Leavitt, at Prof. Ames' suggestion, wrote a monograph on the genus Aeria, a highly scientific paper of great value.

Most Important Books

In 1908 he went to the New Jersey State Normal School, as head of the Biological Department, remaining there twenty years. Since 1928, when he retired, Dr. Leavitt has spent his time in travel and study and in writing his "Forest Trees of New England." Other publications by him are "Roots of Vascular Cryptogams, Monocotyledons and Angiosperms," and "Absorption of Water Vapor by Plants" which has been translated into French and re-published by the principal horticultural journal of Belgium and re-printed in India and Australia.

"Health Training for Teachers," written for and published by the Bureau of Education of the United States, is considered by Dr.

Leavitt his most important work, although he says that in his own eyes his most artistic production is "Effects of Success and Failure on the School Child," which was published in the Journal of Education. "Yes," said he, "the things I have done in education have afforded me the most satisfaction. New Jersey was the first state to have an adequate health law for the schools and I wrote the bill that set up the commission that framed the law." These are only a few of the achievements that led to Dr. Leavitt's being made a Fellow of the American Association for the Advancement of Science, an honor which the members of the association conferred upon him in recognition of contributions to science.

Romance of Blazo Mansion

If you have read Dr. Cornelius Weygandt's charming book on New Hampshire, "The White Hills," you will recall the chapter dedicated to Maude M. Varney called "Love and the Law Long Ago," in which is related the romance of Mr. Blazo and Polly Freeman. Mr. Blazo, the 27-years-old Parsonsfield schoolmaster who fell in love with his pupil, Mary Freeman, of Sandwich, N.H., when she was 15 and married her on December 24, 1835, was Robert Tibbetts Blazo, the grandfather of Dr. Robert Greenleaf Leavitt.

After his marriage Mr. Blazo, who had been admitted to the Strafford County bar in 1830, and had practiced in Moultonborough and Sandwich, moved back to Parsonsfield and bought the family homestead which his uncle William Blazo had built. He and Polly became the parents of four children, one of whom was Susan Blazo. Susan attended the seminary [Parsonsfield Seminary] across the road and there met a young student from Buckfield, J.G. Leavitt, who had come to North Parsonsfield to prepare for Waterville College, now Colby. They fell in love just as Robert and Polly had done, got married and lived in the Blazo mansion with Susan's parents. After a time our Dr. Leavitt was born and now the old house has come to him and he returns from wherever he may be early each summer to spend long restful months in its quiet rooms, filled with books and pictures and rare antiques.

He has always considered North Parsonsfield his home because he was born there and because his family was among the first settlers. It is his legal residence just as it has been of generations of Blazo men before him. First, Amos Blazo, son of William Blazo of Bordeaux, France, who came to this country in 1735 and settled in Greenland, N.H., pioneered in Parsonsfield in 1778. Then Amos's five sons, all of whom settled on nearby farms, William building the mansion which afterward was purchased by the young lawyer, "Mr. Blazo," as Polly Freeman always called him, even after they were married.

And now Dr. Leavitt, with a grandson of his own growing up in the very house in which he spent his own childhood, the Blazo mansion, facing the Sandwich mountains of New Hampshire from beyond whose blue summits came Polly, the bride, close to a century ago.

**John Greenleaf Leavitt (JGL) Principal at Parsonsfield
Seminary (1859) and Congregational Minister in Webster
Massachusetts**

Memoir of *ROBERT GREENLEAF LEAVITT*
By his son Russell Leavitt

This is being written in 1977 by his son, Russell Leavitt. The idea is that one or another person in generations that succeed me may find it of interest--either entertaining or out of curiosity--to read about an ancestor who would otherwise be lost in the mists of time. Part (I) is a short biography which aims to help a reader of my actual recollection in Part (II) to identify times and places which otherwise may well become intermingled and confusing in the telling.

Part (I) Biographical sketch.

RGL was born Sept. 28, 1865 and died in October 1942, both in North Parsonsfield, Maine where he lived much of his life in the big white five-chimneyed house at Blazo's Corner. He was the only offspring of Susan Chapman Blazo and John Greenleaf Leavitt, a Congregational minister, who had been married in the early 1860s. The latter held pulpits in various parts of Maine before his most important one which was in Webster, Mass., where he became intimate friends with the town's principle dry goods merchant, William Towne Shumway. This is worth noting because one of the Shumway daughters was later the bride of RGL and the mother of Russell Leavitt. John G. Leavitt died in 1885; while the Leavitts continued to live in Webster my father attended Worcester [Academy], then went to Harvard College, living in Cambridge. While there he went in for athletics and became intercollegiate pole vault champion as well as a prize-winning jumper. He was graduated AB in June 1889. He taught school at DeVeaux School in

Niagara Falls, N.Y., then at Williston Seminary in Easthampton, Mass. He and Janet Shumway were married in 1890. Their honeymoon trip was delayed (lack of funds?) until 1894 when they made a two-month trip to Europe (a diary kept by my mother tells of the embarking from Montreal on a cattle boat, of bed bugs, of running into ice bergs, of visiting England, Germany, Switzerland and Paris). RGL evidently studied for and took his M and PhD degrees at Harvard in the latter 1890s and the family lived in Cambridge. He wrote "Leavitt's Outlines of Botany," a standard textbook at the time; it was published by the Harvard University Press. He probably did teaching as well for the family did not starve. Around 1900 he became a "partner" in botanical research with Oakes Ames whom he knew at Harvard and who was a wealthy person with his own greenhouse and laboratory (and staff) in North Easton, Mass. It was certainly a partnership so far as research goes but RGL was obviously paid a salary by Ames. Our family moved to Stoughton, Mass. (four miles from North Easton) and it was there in early 1902 that my mother died (pneumonia with tuberculosis in the background). I hardly remember her though I do recall being taken into her bedroom. Dad kept on working with Ames and my grandmother Leavitt was brought in to act as a substitute mother for the next several years. The botanical research centered on orchids. Ames and RGL made one trip to Holland and one to Cuba in pursuit of their subject. A definitive work on orchids was eventually published as the outcome.

In 1906 a marked change occurred in RGL's life. He

married Ida Gertrude Ruggli of Cambridge (graduate of Radcliffe around, probably just before 1900 [1901]) in October. A daughter Constance Ruggli Leavitt was born in 1907 (as it happened eleven years to the day after RL's birthday, on Dec. 19th.) He ended his Ames connection in 1908 and began a new career as head of the department of biology at the New Jersey State Normal School (teacher's college) in Trenton [New Jersey College], to which city the whole family moved in the late summer. This was a change from RGL's relatively closed life of Stoughton where his activities were on a small scale; he had been a member of the Town School Committee and somewhat active in the Congregational Church, but most of his duties were with his family. No social life. Now he became part of the broader, more worldly world. His mother (Grandma Leavitt) retired to Blazo Corner, to which the whole family migrated every summer both then and for years thereafter. [A note should be inserted here about the big house at Blazo's Corner. Grandma Leavitt died there early in 1920. She had owned half of the property and this went to her son under her will. The other half belonged to her sister, "Aunt Emily Browne" who died circa 1930 leaving it to daughter Mrs. Maude [Browne] Varney who in her turn at her death left her share equally to me and brother Bob. Both of us arranged to transfer our shares to RGL and Ida in the 1930s and 1940s.] RGL palpably enjoyed his life in Trenton. He took part in establishing a small Unitarian church there. About 1914 he and Ida bought land in Morrisville, PA, across the river from Trenton. They had a house planned and in due course built there.

This was their residence until he retired from teaching in 1928 and perhaps after that. His two sons had, meantime, gone away to college, (Harvard), then to war and both had jobs in NY City from 1920 onward. Both were married in 1922 and RGL's grandchildren began to arrive on the scene in 1923-24. Constance was being educated; he, himself, was in good health into the 1930s. The three of them made an extensive tour of Europe in 1929. Constance was married in 1931 [1934] and she and her husband lived for the most part near RGL and Ida. RGL suffered painful losses in the stock market crash that began in October 1929 and his health declined during the 1930s--a mastoid operation in Greenwich in 1931 and deterioration of bone structure of the spine later. He continued his studies and in 1932 published a slender Forest Trees of New England." He and Ida lived in Maine and Cambridge, alternating with the seasons, and some of the time in Virginia where Constance's husband's work had moved. She had son Robert in 1936. Dad's summers continued at Blazo's Corner and there he died while walking on the nearby road in 1942, just after his birthday number 77. His body was buried in the near-at-hand family burial ground.

Part II, Personal Recollections Concerning RGL and his doings.

(A) Preface

My recollection of events in my father's life are many and varied. They often make good reading, I hope. All the same, recollections on a piecemeal basis miss something, i.e. the picture as a whole. Therefore I start with concise statements of what he was like as a whole person. Three qualities shine through and surround the details of what he was and did.

(1) All along his persistent aim was to serve others rather than himself.

(2) He was imbued with a stubborn *joie de viore* of his own personal variety. It burst forth intermittently in what he planned and did, not in utterance. It continued as long as he was in good health.

(3) He was held in loving respect and was, throughout his life viewed as the head of his branch of the Leavitt clan.

His individual characteristics were those of a "loner;" he was a quiet person, inventive and creative, a leader only in certain times and under certain conditions. He seemed naive, sometimes unwise in worldly affairs, puritanical, not an easy social personality, conspicuously compassionate toward animals, a "liberal" in viewpoint, tempered by some real prejudices. Such traits are no more mixed or contradictory than one observes in almost any "normal" person.

Part II Personal Recollections etc. (cont.)

(B) Events and their surroundings

My first clear memories of my father come from the period after my mother's death and while Grandma Leavitt was, in effect, my "surrogate" mother. It was a time when people were feeling a clash between long accustomed life styles and the on-rushing modern world. RGL, born in the horse and buggy age, matured in the age of the Iron Horse. Railways were now threading the entire eastern U.S., running, it seemed, headlong, across streets and highways.

An early recollection is of my father making with his own hand-tools a pair of small, play "crossing gates" for brother Bob and me in our own back yard. In real life, crossing gates were placed where rail tracks crossed a busy street or main highway. They were barriers against collisions, lowered when trains were nearing, raised after passage. It is impossible to convey the drama in a small boy's soul if he happened to be at hand when the keeper cranked the gates down. For then came the whistling, bell ringing, steam hissing, altogether clamorous monster while the boy trembled safely behind the gates, both scared and thrilled.

To make a long story short, my father (who must have felt like vibrations in earlier years) placed his small gate models in our sand pile at home where one of us would play locomotive, the other the gate-keeper. The locomotive made as much noise as a boy can and the young actor moved his arms back and forth like piston rods. The drama stamped itself on my memory with RGL back and, as it were, applauding.

It must have been about the same time that RGL and his confrere Ames went to Holland to do some work on orchids. He took brother Bob and me into Boston to see the Cunard liner "Saxonia" on which they were to cross the Atlantic. I cannot forget his showing us over the ship with its great red funnel. But I especially remember his return. It had been notified in advance and

Bob and I were sent walking down Seaver Street in Stoughton to meet him who would be walking up from the station. I can feel his warm embrace and the bristle of his beard when he kissed me. He gave a package to each of us to carry. It turned out that there were colored prints of Holland, framed and destined for house decoration. I remember that these were discovered, on their being opened, to be marked "made in USA," and that he was taken aback. This is worth mentioning only because it shows so clearly his un-worldliness.

Life for young boys in the Leavitt household in those years was marked by Saturday or Sunday afternoon walks with father. In the spring it was searching for the Mayflower in swampy meadows or woods, in other seasons for odd insects or plants. RGL the naturalist, the lover of outdoors.

I have mentioned that he was imaginative and creative. The words come close to describing what he did by way of transporting himself to and from the Ames Laboratory in North Easton, four miles away, where his daily work was. He bought himself the very latest thing in the way of bicycles, a "Columbia Chainless" (species now extinct). It was powered by pedals via a rod encased in metal tubing geared to the back wheel. It was admired in the neighborhood and, except in snowy or icy conditions, Dad covered the eight miles on it daily. He always carried a protection against possible attack by a dog a water pistol filled (i.e. loaded) with ammonia. While he was there in North Easton, it was arranged that Bob and I should go to see him there several times. He was always joyful to see us and took delight in showing us whatever there was to excite or interest young boys. Two men, Tim and Tom, who were staff aides, joined in the fun, demonstrating a monkey swimming in the greenhouse pool, parrots and other exotic birds, etc. with Dad always as an escort. These visits surely reflected him as, looking back now, the lonely widower. Family had more allure for him than botanical study.

In Stoughton my memory recalls sharply RGL as lover of music. He was conductor (and the tenor voice) of the small Congregational church choir. Preparing probably for the next Sunday's service, I can hear him singing in his bath at home: "Fear not! Fear not! For behold I bring you good tidings of great joy...." The choir members presented him, when we left Stoughton for Trenton, with a lovely black baton adorned with some silver. Enjoyment of music ran right through his years. In Trenton we acquired one of those hand-powered phonographs. Its coil spring had to be left well wound up lest its pitch began to sag. And this was replaced in due time by a player piano, foot or leg powered. Recordings on slotted paper rolls produced lovely music as the pumped in air ran through the slots and controlled the keys in a manner still pretty mysterious to me. The pianist (if he could deserve that title) could control fff and ppp with levers at the keyboard. A good deal of what is called classical music came into Leavitt family ears by these crude mechanisms.

But I am getting ahead of my recollections—timing has become disordered in the telling. A great change in the whole family situation, which gave RGL and all of us new life in more senses than one.

The renewed family

In October 1906, Dad married again. And thenceforth a very considerable transformation in his mode of life, that is, in his spirit, came forth. The event itself was before we left Stoughton. Indeed, Constance, who surely symbolizes the change, was born before we moved. But all credit must be given to Ida Ruggli the bride. She was nearly ten years younger than Dad. Her experience had been much more of the great world than was his (she had a job in the office of the widely known Boston law firm, a partner of which became Supreme Court Justice Brandeis). She was one of five sisters of whom only one had married. The arrival of Constance must have introduced a sense of urgency (might not the family increase still further) over and above Ida's realism. She must have made it clear that to continue with Ames would lead to a dead end and I have no doubt she set Dad on a path of a new occupation.

RGL's New Life as Teacher

When in due course, he got the job as head of the department of biology at the state teacher's college (Normal School, then) to start in September 1907, the situation became vivid in my mind through hearing (probably over-hearing) an intra-family conversation in Stoughton. In awestruck tones someone—probably my grandmother-- was being told of the enormous increase in pay which the new job would bring. He was to have a salary of $2,000 a year!

In my memory he obviously enjoyed involvement in the school life. Two small incidents are small illustrations: Here at age of about 45 he was playing baseball for the faculty against the alumni in an annual "fun" game. And what a kick he got out of being asked to be toastmaster at the annual dinner of a women students' sorority, "The Ionians." This was held at Trenton's swank restaurant and the girls had a taxi cab to fetch him downtown and bring him home. He told the family afterward of a rhyme he composed on his way and had recited. About like this:

"Being your guest here my pride it doth tickle
The Ionian belles are certainly 'swells'
I usually come down for a nickel" * (streetcar fare circa 1911)

[*As recalled by my grandmother Ida Leavitt : "The taxi's a stylish vehicle/To ride in it my pride it doth tickle/The Ionian bells /are certainly swells/I usually come down for a nickel" MF]

Trenton and Blazo's Corner

City life was no barrier to his feeling for his friends of the animal world. A small instance: he somehow managed to trap a skunk in our back yard. Maybe it was a baby animal when caught. Anyhow it was given a home at the bottom of a large barrel that stood upright on the back porch where it was fed and tamed. The rest of the family was very much afraid of getting anywhere near, needlessly so. I don't know the fate of the small unattractive animal.

The connection with animals leads me to the story of what I still think was one of Dad's finer exploits. I should explain that our vacations were always at Blazo's corner and that part of his time there was given to what he regarded as in some sense "farming." He bought perhaps 20 acres on the road to Porter, a place with a great barn close to the road near the foot of Churchill's hill, a mile from Blazo's corner. The foregoing will make it clear why a horse was needed—to plow, cut and rake hay, transport RGL, Bob and me, back and forth in a farm wagon.

He met this need in a way few would have considered possible. A Trenton family of some prominence had a Kentucky thoroughbred gelding that served as their coach horse. The time (circa 1909) had come for "Breeze," the horse, to be replaced by an auto. Dad saw clearly that Breeze could become his not very hard worked draft animal in Maine. So he bought no longer young Breeze—and a nice buggy along with him—for that purpose. But this only begins the story.

Dad sent the rest of us on ahead to Parsonsfield and, by himself, drove Breeze and buggy all the way, some 400 or more miles, to join us at Blazo's corner. The journey took two weeks (perhaps more) and one job of horse shoeing en route. His track was northward to Bear Mt. Bridge across the Hudson below Poughkeepsie (just built), thence via the Berkshire Hills to

Greenfield where he stopped a night with the Russell family. And so to Keene, N.H. and eventually, skirting Lake Winnepesaukee on the south, to Ossipee and Blazo's corner. Those were days when autos were becoming nearly commonplace and when longish horse-drawn travel was all but a thing of the past. No wonder RGL's exploit was the talk of the town, locally at least. Breeze was a gentle creature, beloved by us all.

Dad did plant young apple trees on his land, hoping to establish an orchard of "Machintosh Reds." (This scheme never matured; it was aborted by gnawing mice, browsing deer, etc. But in any case it seems clear from another event that his "farming" was, as much as anything else, really an extension of his interest in laboratory work. A wild apple sapling had taken root near the barn. This kindled his imagination (and maybe his sense of fun—what I've called his own private brand of *jore de livre*). Anyhow, he sent off to Orono (Maine State Agricultural Station) for scions of a dozen different varieties of apples known to be hardy in Maine. These he grafted onto a dozen different branches of the young wild apple tree. When the grafts had "taken" and buds began to promise early blooms, still another step had to be taken. It was important, it seems, to make sure that each newly grown blossom be pollenated (I hope that is the right word) by pollen from the same variety (ask me not why!) So he tied paper bags around each prospective producer of fruit and did the fertilizing himself, instead of leaving it to the random work of the bees, tying each one tight again after the work was done. In appearance, thus, the sapling became a tree full of "paper bag fruit and this attracted local farmers or just passers by on the road. RGL was an inventive person, an original thinker and courageous.

His feeling for the joy of life flourished in other ways. In 1909 he took Bob and me on a tramping trip to the White Mountains, indeed to the top of Mt. Washington and home again. The first leg was via Effingham Falls to West Ossipee on a hot summer day. All went well until, passing across the plain north of Lake Ossipee, a thunderstorm came upon us. Dad made us lie down, rods apart, amid low blueberry bushes as the most likely way to avoid lightening. We had just settled down when he jumped up with a shout that scared me. But the alarm went as suddenly as it had come. He had laid himself almost on top of a bee's nest and had taken a fast move to safety with his shout. After a night at an inn in West Ossipee we hiked to and climbed Mt. Chocorua, sleeping the night just below the peak. Thence, our course took us to North Conway where we were joined by Ida's sister Clara (spinster school teacher on vacation). We all took the train through the "notch," left it at Crawfords and started up the trail to the "tip-top house" of Washington. It took us all day—in bright sunshine, mostly above the tree line. Clara was lucky enough to find that the house had one room with a bed available, but we "men folk" slept on what Dad called the "soft-pine" boards of the floor. In the morning, Clara went down by the cog-wheel train, and we three took the "carriage road" as it was then called to the Glen House, walked the 17 miles to Jackson, caught a train to Cornish (Maine) and so walked that 8 miles to Blazo's corner. A long day! RGL loved the whole venture as much as did we youngsters.

In a later year (1914) he and I did the thing over again by a different and wilder route. He was then all but 50 years old. The love of the outdoors, the closeness to nature was still abundantly in him.

Going backward a bit in time (the episode was in 1907) I recall vividly the same traits in Dad—his love of the outdoors, his persistent drive to enjoy life in his own way—also his "creativity." We were at Blazo's Corner. Ida was pregnant with Constance. We had staying with us Clara and, I think, Eva—Ida's sisters. Dad planned a "camp-out" for all of us, including two of Ida's nephews, Leland and Fred Whitney, lads roughly the same age as Bob and me. Yards of unbleached cotton cloth were bought and the ladies spent days in making two large "wall tents." one for the ladies, the other for us gents. The whole apparatus was carted to the Ossipee River bank just beyond the mouth of the South River. There we fished, swam, had cook-outs (by a great fire at night) for maybe four days. Great fun, designed by RGL.

Dad neither smoked nor drank alcohol. But I recall an occasion about 1912 when his high principles were slightly derailed—an accident. He was driving Breeze back from Kezar Falls on a sunny afternoon and passing George Young's house, perhaps half a mile from the Porter Bridge, was hailed by old George who wanted him to come sit on the porch and pass the time of day. Dad did so and gladly sipped some of George's home-made cider as they talked. Delicious it evidently was, with no hint to Dad of its hardness. Anyhow, in due course he arrived at Blazo's Corner red in the face and finding everything pretty funny. Bob and I took care of Breeze. Dad slept it off. It was never spoken of within the family circle.

It wasn't long after that time when Dad, with his persistent vitality, bought some acreage in Morrisville, Pennsylvania, across the Delaware River from Trenton. He and Ida had a house designed in accord with their dreams and, after some delay had a house built there in which they lived for the next ten or fifteen years. It is not easy to fix the dates of the move to Pennsylvania but it had been accomplished by the time Bob and I had gone off to college, i.e. in the autumn of 1913.

These recollections become less ruled by the calendar as my absence at college (and thereafter) inevitably reduced or made more intermittent my direct contact with Dad and the others. RGL had sought (and I am anxious to record this, to instill in me (and Bob) a sense of self reliance and to push us toward maturity. I keenly remember how in September 1911, he encouraged me to apply for and get a day off from school in order to go off alone to Philadelphia (by train, of course) to stand in line and get into the ball park to see a World Series baseball game, the first pro-baseball game I had ever seen. I can still name most of the players on those two famous teams!) Dad's efforts along these lines were persistent. Bob went to N.Y. to work in Uncle Will Russell's office in the summer of 1915 and in the same year I was dispatched to work picking peaches in the renowned peach farm near Waterbury, Connecticut. Then in the 1916 summer I was encourage to work in New York, again with the help of Uncle Will Russell, in whose apartment I lived. I cite these episodes merely to show RGL's unremitting sense of responsibility to get his offspring started in adulthood. With me, I had to be pushed because at that stage I was indeed immature.

1916 was the year of a considerable polio epidemic in the U.S. At the summer's end when Bob and I came to spend a week or so at Blazo's corner, we were met by Dad who, before we were allowed to come inside, made us shed our clothes in the field back of the house, there to bathe and put on something tat hadn't been near the cities. We were thus decontaminated. RGL the family's guardian against peril! RGL the scientist at work!

Trenton and the later years

Here seems to be the place for some speculative thought about R.G.L. I wondered at the time and have ever since about Dad's inner feelings relative to Uncle Will Russell. I was named after him. He had married my mother's elder sister, Kate Shumway (Aunt Kate). Their marriage had only one offspring, a girl (Cousin Janet Russell of Greenfield, at this writing in her 92nd year.) In the light of some of the facts below, he must have yearned for a son for he treated me more or less like a son. Dad had hoped I would be a scientist, perhaps a teacher, possibly a scientific farmer. He

104

suggested going to Cornell and, at another time, to Wisconsin. But Uncle Will's high success as business man acted as a magnet on me and I veered in the business direction. Though not the first of his favors to me, he got me a summer job (1916) in his N.Y. office (International Paper Co.) and for that period I lived in his apartment on West 85th St. The next year he helped me get a discharge from the U.S. Navy (pulling strings with a relative of his) and financed my passage to Europe to join the American Ambulance [Service] with the French Army (I had only one eye and was ineligible for U.S. Army draft—I'd got in the Naval Reserve as an ordinary seaman by a kind of fluke *.) Uncle Will bought clothes, etc. for me for overseas warmth. In postwar years he helped me in both large and small ways. Dad never showed a sign that he might feel badly, that I was being "alienated." I think he had too big a viewpoint for such sentiments. But there was room for some possibly ill feelings on the part of a less honest and generous a person than Dad was. My speculative thoughts were speculative, not engendered by any clear facts.)

The Years of Decline

As for speculation in a different sense, Dad was lured into the stock market in the great boom of 1917-29—just like millions of other people. He was retiring from teaching in 1928 and no doubt did see every reason to fortify his coming years of retirement. I, myself, knew all that seemed to be happening because investment

105

had become my business. But I was living in London where the atmosphere was somewhat less crazy. Letters from a young son couldn't compete with the thrill of joining the crowd that was making fortunes (on paper, at least) at home. Also I was just plain lucky. I had to sell out much in 1928 to get cash to buy an interest in Moody's — in effect a partnership. And when I was moved back to the U.S. in early September 1929, I had to sell all the rest to buy a house in Greenwich. (No rents available, thank goodness.) RGL all but went broke in 1930-31-32. He did have his teacher's pension, and some good, though not many securities. And at some point he sold*the Morrisville house and land. [*The house was actually sold by his widow, my grandmother Ida, in the fall 1948 when we moved to Charlottesville, VA so my mother could attend UVA. The house in Morrisville was my first home, along with Parsonsfield every summer, from 1943 until 1948, and I still remember it in every detail.] Depending on the season, he and Ida and Constance lived in Maine and Cambridge where an apartment was rented. RL made regular contributions, by way of easing their circumstances. At all events they lived without any severe hardship in the thirties.

Meanwhile Dad interested himself in work of the kind he was so well fitted for, writing botanical piece and the "Forest Trees of New England" book. In two summers in the mid-thirties he had grandsons Keith (RKL's eldest) and Scot (RL's eldest), both around 12, as summer "pupils" as well as helpers at Blazo's corner. Constance was married in 1931 [May 12, 1934] in Cambridge. They had son Robert in 1936. She and family lived near to Dad and

106

Ida in Cambridge [and still in the house in Morrisville] and a good deal of time in Maine in the summer.

The one blight in his life—illness--began to develop during the 1930s. Dad had always talked zestfully of living to be 100! In 1931 he had to have a mastoid operation and came to Greenwich where a surgeon friend of RL's did the job—Ida staying in RL's house during the crisis. (Sulfur drugs and antibiotics have since done away with such operations.) Somewhat later Dad began to suffer from deterioration of the bone structure of the spine which to an extent crippled him. Inevitably he was losing his spirits, but he was never in my presence a depressed personality. RL and family, who summered on Lake Kezar, fifty miles or so to the north, drove down to visit him several times and always found him joyful on these occasions.

Close touch tended to fade as the war came on. RL worked in Washington with the War Shipping Administration; RKL was in Maryland, a major in the army. That is where we got word of RGL's death. He was walking on the road between the old house at Blazo's Corner and Maude Varney's, a few hundred feet away when life left him, one might say in a way characteristic of him, quietly and without bothering anyone. His sons came hastily from Washington to join Ida, Constance and young Robert. His body was put to rest in the family graveyard near at hand. During the outdoor service a great flight of war planes passed low overhead on their way to Europe.

Robert Keith Leavitt Writer (1895–1967) *from Wikipedia*

Son of Robert Greenleaf Leavitt

Sherlock Holmes statue, Edinburgh, Scotland. Bob Leavitt, longtime historian, Baker Street Irregulars

Robert Keith Leavitt (1895–1967) was a Harvard-educated New York City advertising copywriter who turned to non-fiction writing. He was the author of many books, including a history of *Webster's Dictionary* and "The Chip on Grandma's Shoulder" (1954.) 'Bob' Leavitt was also the longtime historian of the original The Baker Street Irregulars, devoted to all things Holmesian, about which he wrote in his "The Origins of 221B Worship."[1]

Leavitt was born on August 20, 1895 in Cambridge, Massachusetts to Dr. Robert Greenleaf Leavitt, a Harvard-trained botanist, researcher, author and later college and high school teacher, and his wife Janet.[2] Dubbed "the fiscal Holmes" by another member of the Baker Street Irregulars,[3] Robert Keith Leavitt showed an early aptitude for ferreting out information. He attended the State Model School in Trenton, New Jersey, where his father was teaching, and graduated from Harvard College in 1917. Shortly afterwards, Leavitt joined the armed forces as 2nd Lieutenant in the 302nd Infantry, where he commanded the Prisoners of War Escort Company 223, with custody of 425 German prisoners.[4]

After the war Leavitt returned home, and found work writing copy for a New York City advertising agency. He spent 13 years in advertising, including a stint as Secretary-Treasurer of the Association of National Advertisers, before turning to a career as a freelance writer. From the beginning Leavitt focused on historical, offbeat subjects. He wrote for a range of publications, including a 1933 article for *Business Week* – during the height of the Depression – on *What we shall sell when the upturn comes – and to whom?* [5] Leavitt sold articles to many publications, including *Forum and Century*, *Advertising and Selling*, *The American Magazine*, *Forbes* and others. In 1946 he wrote a 66-page booklet entitled *Your Pay Envelope – and how it gets that way*. To make ends meet, Leavitt wrote corporate histories, including that of the Pennsylvania Salt Manufacturing Company, and he wrote for publications of the Great Northern Railway. The former copywriter also continued to dabble in advertising and public relations.

The corporate biographies Leavitt wrote to garner a

paycheck included titles like *Prologue to Tomorrow: A History of the First Hundred Years in the Life of the Pennsylvania Salt Manufacturing Company* (1950); *Goods Roads* about the General Motors Overseas operations (1949); *Foundation for the Future: History of the Stanley Works* for Stanley Tools (1951); and 1954's *Life at Tung-Sol 1904–1954: An Informal Story of the First Half-century of Tung-Sol Electric Inc*. Leavitt also found time to produce books on lighter subjects, notably *The Chip on Grandma's Shoulder*, a memoir about his Maine grandmother Susan C. (Blazo) Leavitt[6] published by J. B. Lippincott in 1954, and *Common Sense About Fund Raising* (Stratford Press, 1949).

But the book for which Leavitt is remembered is *Noah's Ark, New England Yankees, and the Endless Quest: A Short History of the Original Webster Dictionaries, with Particular Reference to Their First Hundred Years as Publications of G. & C. Merriam Company*. Although a corporate history—published by G. & C. Merriam Company of Springfield, Massachusetts in 1947 -- *Noah's Ark* explores the history of Noah Webster and his competitor Joseph Emerson Worcester. The book's first half examines Webster's life and lexicography; the second half etches the "War of the

Dictionaries", the struggle for supremacy between Webster's and his competitor Worcester's dictionaries. Leavitt laid out the history of Webster's publishing house after its eponymous title was sold to the Merriam family (today's Merriam-Webster).[7]

In *Noah's Ark* Leavitt plumbed the shoals of international lexicography and usage. "In considering the influence of Webster's American Dictionary outside the United States," writes David Micklethwait in *Noah Webster and the American Dictionary*, "Leavitt says that Webster was 'increasingly the arbiter of definitions in British life', until the appearance of John Ogilvie's *Imperial Dictionary* in 1850, 'itself largely indebted to the American source.'"[8] Leavitt's work remains the definitive history of Noah Webster and his legacy.[9]

When not writing articles and books, Leavitt indulged his passion for Sherlock Holmes, helping found, with his friend Christopher Morley, The Baker Street Irregulars, an informal group of Arthur Conan Doyle devotees. Records do not reflect when the author's affinity for Sherlock Holmes began, but his works show he was a close reader of Sir Arthur Conan Doyle's oeuvre.[10] It was in Leavitt's writings as historian of the Irregulars that he seemed most at home, his imagination prowling Arthur Conan Doyle's intricate plots, sniffing for clues about the Scottish-born author and his fictional sleuth. In an article entitled *Annie Oakley in Baker Street*, for instance, Leavitt examined Sherlock Holmes's choice of handgun: Leavitt theorized from Doyle's description that Holmes's sidearm was a Webley Metropolitan Police Model, with 2½-inch barrel – the smallest handgun available, and subject to concealment without a holster.[11]

The voracious Leavitt mined Holmes's adventures for monographs of his own. He authored *The Curious Matter of the Anonymous Latin Epitaph*, *The Cardboard Box* and others. In an essay in *The Baker Street Journal*, the Baker Street Irregulars's periodical,[12] Leavitt thought fit to question the marksmanship of the revered detective. In *Annie Oakley in Baker Street*, Leavitt claimed that Dr. Watson's revolver shot had toppled the villain Tonga from the deck of the *Aurora* into the River Thames, and not Holmes's. In another piece Leavitt explored the hazy question of whether Dr. Arthur Watson had remarried.[13] Leavitt was a frequent contributor to *The Baker Street Journal*, published by Ben Abramson, proprietor of Manhattan's Argus Book Shop and a Holmes aficionado,

112

who published musings of the best-known Sherlockians.

Within the close-knit Irregulars, Leavitt was known for his expertise in ballistics,[14] optics and finances, sometimes combining them to examine the deeds of Conan Doyle's legendary hero.

When not writing about Holmes, Leavitt chose the company of friends like fellow Baker Street Irregulars Christopher Morley and Elmer Davis,[15] as well as other writers, reporters, advertising men and artists of the day. Leavitt had an only brother, Russell Greenleaf Leavitt, who graduated from Harvard College in 1917, and who subsequently received a deferment from the military for poor eyesight. But Russell Leavitt joined the U.S. Navy and eventually wangled an assignment driving an ambulance for the U.S. Army Ambulance Corps during the First World War.[16] Russell Leavitt drove his ambulance on the front lines for 11 months, piloting his vehicle at Verdun and Flanders, and eventually serving in the Chemical Warfare Service Laboratory at Paris.[17]

In a piece called *The Christmas Miracle*, Bob Leavitt recalled tramping through the small Massachusetts town of Stoughton on Christmas Eve at age six with his father Robert and brother Russell, searching for a

Christmas tree. Leavitt's father stopped periodically and cut several tiny balsam seedlings. "Our father was a botanist Ph.D., given to plucking all manner of specimens wherever we walked, with the offhand explanation, '*A fine Tsuga canadensis*, or whatever it was," Leavitt wrote. 'By nightfall we had forgotten all about the walk." At home that evening, wondering about their tree, the two boys were shown a jar of earth devoid of plant life. If they sang 'O Little Town of Bethlehem' particularly well, their mother told them, the trees might grow.

The youngsters left the room, and began to sing. When they looked again, the seedlings had grown a foot. They repaired to the other room and sang some more. When they came back, the trees had grown again. "We went out and tried harder on that song," wrote Leavitt, "and when we re-entered the sitting room, the Tree had grown to perhaps a foot or so in height.... We went out and tried harder on that song. And sure enough this Time the tree was taller than either boy.... To this day I cannot hear 'O Little Town of Bethlehem,' from however cracked a curbside organ, without hearing through and beyond it the clear, true voice of my mother."[18]

Bob Leavitt died at Scarsdale, New York, in 1967.

He was 72. His botanist father had died in 1942 while walking in Parsonsfield, Maine. His mother, Janet (Shumway) Leavitt, died of pneumonia in 1902 when Leavitt was seven.

Quotes[edit]

"People don't ask for facts in making up their minds. They would rather have one good soul-satisfying emotion than a dozen facts."

—Robert Keith Leavitt, *Voyages and Discoveries*, 1939[19]

See also[edit]

• Blazo-Leavitt House

• Robert Greenleaf Leavitt

References[edit]

1 ^ *The Origin of 221B Worship, Sherlock Holmes by Gas-lamp: Highlights from the First Four Decades of the Baker Street Journal*, Philip A. Shreffler, Fordham University Press, 1989 ISBN 0-8232-1221-1 ISBN 978-0-8232-1221-7

2 ^ Secretary's Report, Harvard College Class of 1889, No. IV, Edward W. Wheeler, Cambridge, Mass., 1901

3 ^ Irregular Records of the Early 'forties: An Archival History of the Baker Street Irregulars, page 22,

January 1941-March 1944, Jon L. Lellenberg,
Edgar Wadsworth Smith, Baker Street Irregulars,
Jon L. Lellenberg, Edgar Wadsworth Smith,
Published by Baker Street Irregulars, 1991

4 ^ Thirtieth Anniversary, Harvard College Class of
1889, Eighth Report of the Class Secretary, June
1919

5 ^ *Business Week* magazine, 1933, page 27, McGraw
Hill, New York

6 ^ A Letter from East Stoughton, Stoughton Historical
Society, stoughtonhistory.com

7 ^ *Noah Webster and the American Dictionary*, David
Micklethwait, Published by McFarland, 2005
ISBN 0-7864-2157-6 ISBN 978-0-7864-2157-2

8 ^ Noah Webster and the American Dictionary, David
Micklethwait, Published by McFarland, 2005
ISBN 0-7864-2157-6 ISBN 978-0-7864-2157-2

9 ^ After the Revolution: Profiles of Early American
Culture, Joseph J. Ellis, W. W. Norton &
Company, 2002 ISBN 0-393-32233-5 ISBN 978-0-
393-32233-0

10   ^ Robert Keith Leavitt in Morley's Studio, Photo,
The Standard Doyle Company: Christopher Morley

on Sherlock Holmes, Christopher Morley, Steven Rothman, Fordham University Press, 1990 ISBN 0-8232-1292-0 ISBN 978-0-8232-1292-7

11 ^ *Ms. Holmes of Baker Street: The Truth about Sherlock*, C. Alan Bradley, William Antony S. Sarjeant, University of Alberta, 2004 ISBN 0-88864-415-9 ISBN 978-0-88864-415-2

12 ^ The Baker Street Irregulars began publishing *The Baker Street Journal*, "an irregular quarterly of Sherlockiana", in 1946.

13 ^ *In Bed with Sherlock Holmes: Sexual Elements in Arthur Conan Doyle's Stories of the Great Detective*, Christopher Redmond, Published by Dundurn Press Ltd., 1984 ISBN 0-88924-142-2 ISBN 978-0-88924-142-8

14 ^ The Standard Doyle Company: Christopher Morley on Sherlock Holmes, by Christopher Morley, Steven Rothman, Fordham University Press, 1990 ISBN 0-8232-1292-0 ISBN 978-0-8232-1292-7

15 ^ Don't Let Them Scare You: The Life and Times of Elmer Davis, by Roger Burlingame, published by Lippincott, 1961, p.10

16 ^ Harvard Alumni Bulletin, Vol. XX, Number 1, Harvard Alumni Association, Harvard Bulletin Inc., Boston, Mass., 1917

17 ^ Harvard College Class of 1889, Thirtieth Anniversary, 1889-1919, Eighth Report of the Class Secretary, June, 1919

18 ^ The Christmas Miracle, Robert Keith Leavitt, Christmas: A Time for Family, Lois L. Kaufman, Illustrated by Barbara Chiantia, Peter Pauper Press, Inc., 1998 ISBN 0-88088-403-7 ISBN 978-0-88088-403-7

19 ^ Dictionary of Quotations in Communications, Lilless McPherson Shilling, Linda K. Fuller, Greenwood Publishing Group, 1997 ISBN 0-313-30430-0 ISBN 978-0-313-30430-9

Further reading[edit]

• *Noah's Ark, New England Yankees, and the Endless Quest: A Short History of the Original Webster Dictionaries, with Particular Reference to Their First Hundred Years as Publications of G. & C. Merriam Company*, Robert Keith Leavitt, Noah Webster, Published by G. & C. Merriam Co., Springfield, Mass., 1947

- *The Chip on Grandma's Shoulder*, Robert Keith Leavitt, Published by Lippincott, Philadelphia, Penn., 1954
- *Common Sense about Fund Raising*, Robert Keith Leavitt, Published by Stratford Press, New York, 1949

LOVE LETTERS
OF MARY (POLLY) FREEMAN AND ROBERT BLAZO

(Transcribed by Mary Freeman, their great, great granddaughter)

First, the letter from Robert Blazo to Polly Freeman, dated August 25--1828

Dear Fedelia,

May some guardian angel direct my pen while I indite these few lines for her, whom holy spirits love with tenderness and compassionate regard. Then we part, yes, Fedelia for a short time to pursue different paths of knowledge. You to pursue those academical studies which ever delight the industrious student and discover to the enquiring mind new beauties, and new stimulants to exertion.--I to plod my weary way up the steep & rugged path of Jurisprudence, where scarcely a flower is seen to delight the weary eye or a purling rill to cool the surrounding atmosphere.-- Those days, which I passed at the academical Institutions of our beloved country flew hapily and swiftly away. --I never again expect to enjoy days so happy as those; so devoid of care; so free from guile and deceit--and so fraught with pleasing anxiety and anticipation. But harken to a Friend. As you value life be careful of your health.--Do not let celebrations of the evening detain you too long from your necessary rest, but retire in season... Long watchings will fade the color of your cheeks; give you a palid countenance and create a faint disagreeable feeling. Make it a rule to retire at ten and rise at five- then you will have the morning air which is pure and bracing.- -Morning walks are far preferable to evening walks.- Exercise is of great importance to one while at school.

--Another thing my Dear girl you will be among strangers therefore you should be careful with whom you associate.-- People will in a great measure, form their good or ill opinion of you as you frequent good or ill company.--and I should advise you to form no intimacies or friendships till a long acquaintance has made thorough proof of their good intentions and amiable dispositions.--Many an innocent girl by not taking proper precaution has been led astray to the injury of her character and to the great affliction of her friends. Never listen a moment to the flattery of a gentleman, for be assured he either has some designs upon you or wishes to be flattered in turn--Never suffer yourself to be out of an evening, without some approved female friend with you for it will give room for talk: "A good name is like precious ointment"--When in company with any one or with many, should anything be advanced offensive to female modesty, do not even countenance it by a smile should all the females present, but show a suitable degree of indignation by a proper behaviour; thus you will secure to yourself respect and a degree of independence--you should suffer no gentleman to take any liberties with you at any time whatever especially when in his company alone, as such things often happen but should he attempt it--rebuke him and should he persist flee from him as you would from one who would destroy your peace and happiness--

Many more things I might say to you but your good sense

will point out the proper path in which you should walk--and in which I believe you wish to walk--I do not write these things to impose them on you as rules but it is sometimes pleasant to have a friend at hand upon whose sincerity we can depend and especially if that friend is older than ourselves and can give advise worthy of attention.

Evening and morning witnesseth my supplications for your welfare and prosperity in this world; and O! may God take you under his special care and protection--May he direct your feet into the paths of virtue and piety and make you like Mary anciently, who sat at the feet of Jesus and received the sweet words of his mouth--

So ever prays your constant friend and--

Constantius

(This is a letter from Polly Freeman to Robert Blazo written the following year--she would have been seventeen at the time.)

Sandwich, May 1, 1829

Mr. Blazo

I do feel very grateful for the explanation I have received of yours of the 27th of March that, I will possess your friendship I thought I might reasonably infer from the manner and the matter of your letter. Receiving three letters written in such rappid succession, the latter of the three so intirely different in style & sentiment from the others & having never received a letter from you of the kind before made me conclude, at once that the latter arose from feelings the very reverse of those which the others possessed, I considered it intended for sarcasm. I felt myself greatly insulted & was in consequence much offended. An insult from one whose prosperity & happiness was (and still is) as dear to me as my own, one whom I can truly say I trusted as the best friend I possess on earth, was more than I could support at least with any degree of ease.

It was the contempt which I thought the contents of your letter manifested & that alone, which influenced me and caused me to answer it in the manner I did. Had it been all that I imagined it to be, I confess with a sorowful heart that I erred greatly in the manner of answering it, that there were many observations which were contrary to my better feelings & occasioned much regret but could not be recalled; for in about twenty four hours from the time I received yours the answer was in the Post office. I had thought a long time before I received your last that it was my duty to proffer my friendship to you let it meet with whatever return it.

All I now can do, is to ask your pardon & that alone will not suffice, but the pardon of Him whose all-seeing eye searches the inmost recesses of our hearts. At the time I answered your letter two opposite passions (Love & Resentment) were contending within my bosom & each by turns prevailed. It was the latter which prompted me to make those expressions which I have had so much reason to regret. For giving way to resentment I condemn myself. But alas! When shall I be enabled to govern my passions? When shall I learn to be wise? As soon as I reflected on the numerous instances in which you had formerly manifested your friendship to me by those friendly precepts & good advice which I am confident has enabled me to avoid many a snare into which I might otherwise have fallen had I not received those admonitions (although I am guilty of many improprieties & errors, frailties & weaknesses) and the polite treatment I had ever received from you, these reflections, extinguished every particle of resentment & gave way to better feelings, to gratitude, and regret for having doubted your former sincerity, whatever might be your present feelings.

You say you have no recollection of having mentioned that I had committed any crime, or of having insinuated any such thing. I thought from one sentence that you quoted "mind with whom you ride S--a for a girl is known by the company she keeps. She should never be seen with suspicious characters especially if their reputation has been (?) in regard to the ladies" that you insinuated that I frequented such company and my character might be judged by that. I thought you said as much as to say that you doubted my chastity. Had you in reality thought as much as I thought you insinuated, there surely must have been some necessary reconciliation between you and me. I do not mention this because I still feel dissatisfied but merely to explain what I have formerly written.

The assertion in the last, that I ever placed implicit confidence in you, I now confirm. You ask if it was not shaken last June while you were at Meredith. I answer it was not. I then considered you the same true friend that I always had from the commencement of our intimate acquaintance. I did not think you had always professed a greater regard for me than you really possessed I could then place as much confidence in you as I ever had & believed that confidence would not be abused. Since you have construed my treatment toward you after you came from Meredith so erroneously, I shall endeavor to explain the cause of it as clearly, as possible. In the interview we had at my uncle French's before you went to Sandwich, you mentioned, that you thought of taking a tour to N. York. I thought you were serious in making the observation. I do not recollect that you told me particularly of the length of time you should be gone, but I was informed by several persons who said they had heard you say it was uncertain but probably some considerable length of time. The thought of your leaving this small part of the world was very unpleasant to me, not from the idea I should be forgotten or should lose your friendship by the means but from the uncertainty of Life and Health it was not improbable we should never meet again. Although you joked me considerably upon my melancholly appearance at our meeting after you came from Meredith, I was ashamed to discover my weakness by telling you the cause, & should not now, but you have construed my actions so erroneously & cannot forbear. I know you asked me if I had heard any unpleasant reports concerning you. After I assured you I had not, you told me to never give myself any uneasiness concerning you when absent, for if there was any change in your feelings toward me you would inform me of it and endeavour to treat me honorably. I did not doubt this in the least before.----I know not from what you should take the idea that my confidence in you, was shaken last fall when you were at Gilmanton. If it was from anything in the letter you received from me, you certainly understood me in a manner differently from what I intended. I was much disappointed in not receiving a call from you because I had anticipated it: for cousin Otis told me the evening you came from Gilmanton I might expect a call from you the next morning. I did not attribute your not calling to indifference, by any means, but expected there was some other reasonable excuse and expected Otis would tell me what it was but he did not see fit to give me any reason.

The sentence in which I spoke about the manner of our parting if I am not greatly deceived was this, I had flattered myself should we ever part it would be in friendship. You say you infer from this, that I had made up my mind we should part, but wished to keep you along until I had made sure of some other, or if I could not get any body else I would take you. Among the catalogue of my sins I trust duplicity has not as yet been numbered, and may He whose kind hand has ever been extended to protect me, although I have so often rebelled against him & have been so ungrateful for his innumerable blessings ever preserve my heart unsullied by it. I have never felt assured we should never part; that our intimacy would ever be continued. Why should I? For you have often told me you should make me no promise. Furthermore, I have heard you say it in former times, that had a lady received your addresses for some considerable length of time, and you should afterwards meet with one whom you thought more capable of rendering you happy than the one with whom you had so long been intimate, you should not consider it your duty to marry her; that you should not only be injuring yourself by the means but her; by giving your hand where you could not bestow your heart. As strong as my affections have ever been for you, I trust I have never been so selfish as to wish to imbitter your future hours by having you marry me, should you find one more worthy of your affections (which I think would be no great task) and one you thought would render your life happier than I could, even could I withhold you and know the parting would render the remainder of my life miserable. For my own part I have felt established. I have thought and still think that I have that confidence of your worth and appreciate it and your friendship so highly that I believe never wished for another's love, or a better friend, excepting Him whose love as far exceeds men's love as the heavens are above the earth. I am not only willing you should know my past feelings toward you, but my present feelings. I now extend the hand of friendship as cheerfully as I ever did and you stand as high as ever in my estimation. Although I was much offended at the contents of your letter, it did not alienate my affections for you nor occasion one wish for another's love.--You said "as for ladies I am done with them till I can find one that will me suit me and place some confidence in what I tell her." From this sentence I infered that you had not as yet found one who suited you, nor one who you thought had placed any confidence in you and likewise that you never intended to call on me again. I thought you were regardless of my feelings or rather, wished and intended to injure them greatly. It was this idea that prompted me to make that cruel observation that you wished to trample me in the dust. Oh, in pity pardon! I do not think you ever wished to abuse me. I do not think if my soul and body were consigned to you, you would intentionally injure me in word, thought, or deed. You have ever treated me with the greatest politeness, and ever manifested a lively interest in my welfare, for which I feel very grateful. The debt of gratitude which is your due from me is very great. Oh! That I might be blessed with the means of making you some acceptable returns. But should I never, I trust you will have your reward. ---How short sighted am I! How greatly have I erred! How egregiously have I been deceived in the meaning of the contents of that letter which occasioned me so much unhappiness and so greatly to err. The thought is truly painful. I trust your generosity will make some allowance for me, as I have erred in a great measure through ignorance. May each sad lesson I have to learn from experience prove a useful one. -- To know that I still possess your friendship produces pleasure intermingled with pain; pleasure, that I have not lost so worthy a friend, and pain, that I am so unworthy of such a blessing. A call from you would surely afford me exquisite pleasure. I wish again to meet the look of approbation, to hear my pardon fall from your own lips. May I never again be left to injure the best of friends.

Your sincere but unhappy

friend,

Mary Freeman

P.S. I cannot at present make so great a sacrifice as to return your letters, unless you should insist upon it. --I am highly gratified to have you correct my errors in writing & hope it will prove an advantage to me by making me more critical. You will however find many errors in this &, but little sense. May you pass an indulgent eye over its weakness & pardon its tedious length.--- Whatever is my fate--may your path through life be strowne with the sweetest flowers and you possess that happiness which will bloom and ripen in eternity

is the sincere wish of your very affectionate

Mary

Constance Ruggli (Leavitt) Hanson

Constance Ruggli (Leavitt) Hanson was born December 19*, 1907, died April 8, 1998 in Portland, Oregon. She will be greatly missed by her family and friends, who will always remember her humor, her love of travel and politics, her zest for romance, adventure and enterprise, her fine writing, her active patriotism, and her lifelong enjoyment of tennis and swimming, sports she pursued well into her eighties. Her grandchildren always found her a willing partner in adventure, a sympathetic listener and, above, a personal advocate. Scorning convention, she generated excitement in new, self conceived plans, and in the face of obstacles presented an almost inexhaustible optimism. She responded to disappointment with imagination, courage, and a great sense of humor, the lasting impression of which, on all who knew her, being perhaps her greatest legacy. The delight she felt and passed on to others in the presence of beauty, especially natural beauty, was ingenuous and always captivating.

A native of Parsonsfield, Maine and a direct descendant of North Parsonsfield's first settler Amos Blazo, she lived in the house she inherited from her ancestors, still standing, opposite Parsonsfield Seminary at what is historically known as Blazo Corner, for 66 years, until she sold it in 1973, not without considerable regret. Her grandchildren were the eighth generation to live on the land and the sixth to live in the house; her cousins, also descended from the Blazos, still live in the house across the road next to the little one-roomed schoolhouse, the Blazo School. While she lived, it remained her dream to someday return to her home in North Parsonsfield.

Daughter of Harvard botany professor Robert Greenleaf Leavitt and Ida (Ruggli) Leavitt, Radcliffe, '01, she was herself a perennial student, attending Harvard Summer School, Pembroke,

Simmons, the University of Oregon, University of Washington, and the University of Virginia in pursuit of a Bachelor's degree, and the University of Maine in Orono for a Master's degree in English history. Her thesis, being published this year, compares the ideas of John Preston, a 17th c. English Puritan minister, with those of Hocking and Jung, disclosing Preston's belief that political action is a religious duty. Certainly she more than considered this idea theoretically, for she regularly partook of political activism herself. A self described arch-conservative, she boldly tore down SDS banners and signs at Harvard during the student riots there in the late 60s, the very prototype of a "little old lady in tennis shoes." Earlier, in the 50s, she had enthusiastically waged war on communists, socialists, liberals, and other "fellow travelers" wherever she found them, though she resigned from the John Birch Society, of which she was an early member, disenchanted with the organization by the mid 60s. Always an avid advocate of free enterprise, she attempted in the early 70s to start a small, fresh water mussell operation on her land on the Ossipee River in Porter, with an AAUW grant. Though it failed, her effort was remarkable and typical of her--she was in her seventies at the time. A fourth generation Unitarian, her religious liberalism seemed at odds with her political conservatism to all but those who understood the complexity and strength of her personal convictions.

She was married twice, both times to Hodge Jackson Hanson, landscape architect for the National Park Service, who died in 1997. The couple married first in 1934, and again (after a thirty-five year

133

hiatus) in 1988 when she was 80 and he was 84, residing briefly in Islesboro and Monroe, Maine before moving out to Oregon to live near their son. They were married in total thirty years.

She is survived by her son Robert Jackson Hanson of Portland, Oregon, who was with her when she died; and daughter Mary ("Mimi" Hanson) Freeman, of Monroe, Maine. She leaves ten grandchildren, Robert's son Joshua Hanson of Portland, Oregon, and Mary's nine children: Eve R. Wentworth of Brookline, Massachusetts, Rachael (Wentworth) Eastman of Chatham, New Hampshire, Donna Wentworth of Somerville, Massachusetts, Erika Wentworth of Richmond-upon- Thames, UK, and Steven Wickham, Joseph Wickham, John Wickham, Andrea Wickham, and Margaret Wickham, all of Monroe, Maine. She also leaves one great grandchild, Alix Louise Wentworth Kalaher, of Richmond-upon-Thames, UK.

She will be interred this summer in the family cemetery in North Parsonsfield, Maine at Blazo Corner, where a service will be held by her family members, relatives, and friends.

* My mother and her half brother Russell Leavitt had the same birthday (December 19th) and called each other twins, though they were eleven years apart in age and had different mothers (Janet Shumway, RGL's first wife, and Ida Gertrude Ruggli, RGL's second wife). My mother and her brother were very close--she called him "Bussie" (for Russell) and he taught her how to fox trot. I corresponded with my Uncle Russell for many years--he was a mentor and a friend.

134

Constance Ruggli Leavitt at 808 Crown St., Morrisville,

Pennsylvania around 1927.

Constance in 1908, about a year old

Constance skiing either in Parsonsfield or Morrisville

Constance sitting with her graddaughters Erika and Donna in 1973
on the south steps.

Constance in Parsonsfield with her parents Robert and Ida Leavitt

Constance with her granddaughters (l-r) Donna and Erika around 1975

Constance watching me skipping rocks at Lake Chocorua
around1952

Printed in Great Britain
by Amazon